Native River

Native River

The Columbia Remembered

William D. Layman

WSU
PRESS

Washington State University Press
Pullman, Washington

The WSU Press and William D. Layman gratefully acknowledge the
support and assistance of the following groups and organizations:

Chelan, Douglas, and Grant County Public Utility Districts

Wanapum Band of Priest Rapids

Colville Confederated Tribes

Wenatchee Valley Museum and Cultural Center

Washington State University Press
PO Box 645910
Pullman, WA 99164-5910
Phone: 800-354-7360
Fax: 509-335-8568
E-mail: wsupress@wsu.edu
Web site: www.wsu.edu/wsupress

Library of Congress Cataloging-in-Publication Data

Layman, William D., 1946-
   Native river : the Columbia remembered : Priest Rapids to the international boundary / William D. Layman.
     p. cm.
   Includes index.
   ISBN 0-87422-258-3 (alk. paper) - ISBN 0-87422-257-5 (pbk. : alk. paper)
   1. Columbia River—History—Anecdotes. 2. Columbia River—History—Pictorial works. 3. Columbia River Valley—History, Local. 4. Folklore—Columbia River.
   I. Title.

F853.L66 2002
979.7—dc21
          2002008244

All royalties from the sale of *Native River* are assigned to the Native River Fund, managed by the Wenatchee Valley Museum and Cultural Center. The purpose of this fund is to develop a collection of exhibit-quality photographs and associated materials for the use and benefit of the Wanapum Band of Priest Rapids, the Colville Confederated Tribes, and the people of the State of Washington.

Cover: Upper Kettle Falls, with Hayes Island in the background.
Frank Palmer, Kettle Falls Public Library

Title page: Kettle Falls.
Washington State University Libraries

Dedicated to
Susan Evans, and to Sage Woman,
who rubbed aromatic leaves upon her feet.
It meant we would stay to learn what the
land and river might teach us.

Family gathering at Rock Island Rapids.
Thomas Grosvenor Collection, Wenatchee Valley Museum and Cultural Center

Native River

The Columbia Remembered

Acknowledgements

Rufus Woods Lake, 1999.
William D. Layman

Columbia River, 1891.
National Archives (77H 615 P-33)

The photographs, documents, and stories comprising this book are, perhaps, somewhat akin to the great stacked lava flows that comprise the spectacular cliffs near Vantage, Washington; each layer possesses its own unique composition and qualities. Interestingly, one of these basalt formations is named the Museum Layer. I find this reference to be a fitting place to begin my acknowledgements.

A number of Washington State museums have generously provided access to their collections. One in particular stands out: the Wenatchee Valley Museum and Cultural Center, formerly known as the North Central Washington Museum. I am indebted to former director William Steward, and to the present director, Keith Williams, along with Heritage Reference Center curator Mark Behler for the trust and patience they have shown me through the years. My heartfelt acknowledgement also extends to another museum member, the late Kirby Billingsley. A key figure in the Public Utility District movement both at the regional and national levels, Kirby was an original Columbia River enthusiast. Whenever the museum needed financial support for acquiring a photograph or map, I only had to ask. His son, Sam, also now deceased, continued this support after his father's passing.

Two other institutions deserve major credit. The Washington State Historical Society and the Center for Columbia River History will forever have my loyalty and support. The respective directors, David Nicandri and William Lang, believed in the importance of this work and offered encouragement for its completion.

A number of historical societies, libraries, archives, government agencies, universities, and small town entities constitute another layer of my acknowledgements. I have found that archivists and librarians are eager to be of service to an amateur historian. Consistently, their professionalism and enthusiasm have made researching this topic a joy. Those who provided major assistance include Joyce Rolstad of the Seattle District of the U.S. Army Corps of Engineers; Joyce Justice of the Seattle Branch of the National Archives; William Erwin of Duke University's Rare Book, Manuscript and Special Collections Library; Trevor Bond of Washington State University's Manuscripts, Archives, and Special Collections; Wilfred Woods of the *Wenatchee World*: Joan Nullet of the Kettle Falls Public Library; Nancy Compau of Spokane Public Library; Marion Garvey of the Stevens County Historical Society; Nicolette Bromberg of Special Collections at the University of Washington; and Rayette Wilder of the Northwest Museum of Arts and Culture. Thanks as well to Brent Cunderla and Gary Webster who taught me the geology I needed to know. Special acknowledgement is due those individuals who generously allowed me to use photographs from their private collections. I wish also to thank Chris Thorsen of Cascade Graphics, who calmly guided me through the labyrinth of digital technology so that I could realize the vision for this book.

For years I knew I needed to write this book, but struggled with the issue of how I could find the time to do it justice. My gratitude goes to Gene Sharratt of the North Central Educational Service District for encouraging me to approach the Chelan, Douglas, and Grant County Public Utility Districts for funding. I remember my trepidation in meeting with various PUD commissioners for fear they would find my proposal not to their liking. What I discovered instead is that the commissioners hold a great fondness for the river and embrace the PUDs' role as river stewards.

I remember a meeting when a question arose relating to the current debate about removing the Snake River dams. Would showing photographs of the pristine Columbia lead people to push for the removal of the dams along the main Columbia too? The commissioners' response was unequivocal: "The river belongs to us all." They assured me that the information included in this book was a part of the river's rich legacy—the story needed telling. My sincere thanks to the Chelan, Douglas, and Grant County Public Utility Districts and the commissioners—particularly Vera Claussen, Mike Doneen, and Barbara Tilly—for the encouragement and support they have provided.

There have been other layers of relationships that have enhanced my own education and understanding. Primary among these are longstanding associations with certain Native American people. I am particularly grateful to Adeline Fredin, Director of the History and Archaeology Department of the Colville Confederated Tribes; William and Matthew Dick of P'squosa (Wenatchi) descent; Tom Louie of the Lost River People; as well as the following Wanapums from Priest Rapids: Bobby Tomanawash, Rex Buck, Arlene Buck Miller, and Lenora Buck Seelatsee. Each has immeasurably deepened my own sensitivities regarding the river and the legacy left by generations of indigenous people. The footprints of these mentors are all over this work.

I am deeply grateful to have been blessed by the spirit and presence of Meridel LeSueur. Likewise, both Gary Snyder and Barry Lopez have influenced me beyond measure, and John Brown and Dr. Robert Ruby stand as giants in our region. Their book *Ferryboats on the Columbia River* is a must-read for those interested in knowing the Columbia as it was. Leigh Marymor, James Donaldson, and Dr. Russell Congdon each have played a special role in moving me out of my unknowing.

It is a pleasure to acknowledge friends who joined me on various river adventures. You have been generous with your support, offering needed encouragement along the way. I feel fortunate to live in a watershed place of relationships where so many people are doing vital work on behalf of the river.

These acknowledgements rest on a foundation of love and support given to me by my partner and wife, Susan Evans. This extends as well to her parents, Chuck and Allie Evans, as well as to my own parents, Byron and Ruth Layman, who provided a supportive environment where I could discover that a life linked to purpose is a life well lived. I also offer thanks to my son Nathan, daughter Gena, and goddaughter Noe Marymor. It means a great deal that they remained curious about how the book project was proceeding and offered their love and support along the way.

Lastly, I thank the Washington State University Press for undertaking the publication of my manuscript; for the patience and expertise of editor Glen Lindeman; for the understanding of coordinator Jean Taylor, who with great sensitivity and care handled my questions through the birthing of this book. And I thank Nancy Grunewald, editor and compositor, who lent her discerning eye and professional skill preparing text, photos, and figures for the book's final published form.

Preface

Native River tells the story of the middle portion of the Columbia River from Priest Rapids to the International Boundary. In the late 19th century, the river here was known as the Upper Columbia, a term now used to designate the river from the International Boundary to its headwaters in British Columbia, Canada.

My interest in the Mid-Columbia began in 1983 with a search for photographs of historic Rock Island Rapids, located thirteen miles below Wenatchee, Washington. I wanted to know this particular place, as it was an Indian petroglyph site of enormous significance before the building of Rock Island Dam. As old photographs came to my attention, I experienced a tinge of excitement; such images brought me closer to walking on the island in my imagination. One day, while visiting the U.S. Army Corps of Engineers' Seattle office, my interest in the river suddenly expanded. As Engineering and Records staff member Joyce Rolstad carefully unrolled a canvas-backed photograph of Rock Island Rapids taken in 1891, I knew I had found something special. Finally, I could see the entire island in one image. Another exhilarating discovery accompanied this visit: I learned that the Rock Island picture was just one of 145 photographs taken of the Columbia that same year. I immediately set about finding as many of them as possible. Clues as to their possible whereabouts emerged as I combed through old engineering reports and records. An 1893 Department of the Army survey reported that a set of 40 views was sent for display to the 1894 Chicago World's Fair. Some were found at the Still Pictures Division of the National Archives and others at the William Perkins Library at Duke University. To date, 88 of these photographs have been located in archives around the country. Meanwhile, the search brought other significant photograph collections to my attention, which I incorporated into various river-related projects, the most significant being a 1988 children's exhibit, "The Upper Columbia...As It Was," sponsored by the North Central Washington Museum in Wenatchee. Through the years, many individuals and institutions have offered support and encouragement in my quest to see this part of the river as it used to be.

From time to time, I carry copies of old photographs to the Columbia's shore to find a photographer's vantage point when taking the historic pictures. Often this requires scrambling over loose rock or traveling by boat to access certain locations. In each instance the effort has resulted in seeing the river in ways I had not known. For this I feel grateful. I hope that *Native River* may deepen and enrich people's sense of their relationship to the river and the landscapes through which it flows. I hope as well that the generations of children to come will increasingly benefit from knowing and honoring the native Columbia.

Orienting oneself to a river that has changed as much as the present-day Columbia can be challenging, often requiring a kind of mental gymnastics. When identifying the side of the river where a photograph was taken, it is logical to think that using east and west would suffice. The Columbia, however, at times flows in a westerly direction with its banks consequently being to the north and south. I have used the terms "right and left bank" to address this issue. Right bank is the right side of the river as one faces downstream; left bank is the opposite side. Is the photograph shown on the next page taken from the right bank looking downriver or the left bank looking upriver? Without knowing the particular nuances of the river and its landscapes, it is impossible to tell. In this instance, the photographer stood on the left bank of the Columbia looking upriver

Condon's Ferry Crossing, left bank looking upriver, ca. 1915.
Frank Palmer, Northwest Museum of Arts and Culture

maps, surveys, books, and agencies seem to count Columbia river miles differently. I use the River Mile Index published by the Pacific Northwest River Basins Commission in 1972.

The Columbia River is our commons. We share its story, yet aspects of the story are sensitive. The first section of the book describes a number of Native American petroglyph and pictograph sites. Pictographs and petroglyphs are vulnerable to natural weathering as well as human impact. With one exception, the eleven sites described in this book have either been completely destroyed or are deep beneath the backwaters of Mid-Columbia dams. Buffalo Cave, the only site not inundated, is protected by the State of Washington's Department of Fish and Wildlife. Petroglyphs removed from their original locations may be seen at Priest Rapids, Ginkgo State Park, the Wenatchee Valley Museum and Cultural Center, and Rocky Reach and Wells dams.

as he headed north on a road leading to Wild Goose Bill Condon's ferry near Parson Rapids (p.118). To aid in orientation, small maps with arrows are included at appropriate places to assist the reader in knowing the vantage point of the photographer.

Also, the term "river mile" at the bottom of some pages refers to the distance of a particular place from the mouth of the Columbia. Various

Not only are pictographs and petroglyphs vulnerable to vandalism, the images can be misused too. The pictographs and petroglyphs of the Mid-Columbia belong to the descendants of the people who made them. The images included in this publication are not to be copied or used in any way or form without the express permission of the proper Native American authorities. My practice always has been to share my research first with members of native groups. The pictograph and petroglyph images included in *Native River* are printed with their knowledge.

Bridgeport, 1999.
William D. Layman

Bridgeport, ca. 1910.
Alfred S. Witter, Melba Cannon Collection

Introduction

Few, if any, people living at the beginning of the 21st century have seen and remember the "entire" expanse of the Columbia River when it ran wild and free. Memories of the un-regulated river now flow like the modern Columbia itself, segment to segment, reservoir to reservoir, with each section of the stream having its own constituency of elders who knew a particular section's untamed waters—the rapids, currents, back eddies, and falls—now vanished from our view.

The number of people who can recall some of these places is rather small. To claim memory of Rock Island Rapids, eliminated in 1931, a person at the time of this writing likely would be more than eighty years old. He or she probably grew up in or near Wenatchee and, in all likelihood, passed the island in the late 1920s while traveling on the new road that headed south to Quincy. Also, a number of people may have briefly seen Rock Island Rapids from a Great Northern passenger car window as a train made its way from Seattle or Spokane. I know of only one living person who remembers taking a boat to the island to see its many petroglyphs. The last person who ran the rapids in a rowboat, Christine Fowler, died in 1999. She was 96.

The story at Kettle Falls is different. Ask any longtime northeast Washington resident, and you are likely to hear a story about seeing the falls. Many speak with excitement of having watched Indians spear salmon from scaffolds suspended precariously over jagged rocks and rushing water. Martin Louie, a Colville Native American born in 1906, remembers fishing from those platforms. Even so, anyone having memories of the falls must be getting on in years. Most have passed their seventieth birthday.

Some places were only rarely seen due to their remote locations. I have encountered only a handful of people who remember Box Canyon before it was flooded by the waters behind Chief Joseph Dam. To visit this secluded spot along the river required both effort and purpose. Without a motorboat, it still does today.

Entire cultures now living within the region have had but little exposure to the natural river. The first large influx of Hispanics, the *braceros,* came into the area following the outbreak of World War II. While a number of early immigrant and resident Latinos may have had an opportunity to see sections of the original Mid-Columbia between Priest Rapids and Grand Coulee, only a very few saw the river above Grand Coulee Dam, which was flooded by 1941.

For a couple of decades following 1860, Chinese miners had a significant presence on the river. In fact, in some localities their population exceeded that of white immigrants. By the turn of the century, their numbers had diminished dramatically. Wong Fook Tai, who died in his small dugout home eighteen miles south of Kettle Falls in 1937, was the last of his generation to live along the river. Many nationalities representing Asian cultures have since come to the area, but like so many others, most Asiatic people never knew the river before hydro development.

Few of the earth's great rivers have undergone such a colossal transformation. While people of the 19th century knew the Columbia primarily for its life-sustaining salmon runs and as a transportation route, people of the 20th century experienced the river more for its capacity to be put to work generating electricity and irrigating vast tracks of land, and for the need to protect homes and businesses from its floods. These enormous changes occurred within an eye blink of time, beginning with Rock Island Dam (completed 1933) and ending with Wells Dam (completed 1967). The building of these dams represents one of the great engineering marvels of the past century.

Many who reflect on what the untamed Columbia once was like express a desire to revisit the river as it was, if only for a day. Opportunity to do just that occurred at Kettle Falls in 1969 and 1974. The spectacle of the re-emerging falls, occasioned by reservoir drawdowns in order for work to proceed on the third powerhouse at Grand Coulee Dam, attracted viewers for miles around. They likely will speak of it for years to come.

Those who knew the river of old, speak about it with awe and respect. Impressed by the Columbia's enormity and presence, they remember its power, its sudden surges, and the particular way its current flowed into whirlpools and back eddies. Respect is always evident, too, born from knowledge of the river's dangerous possibilities.

Native river people whose lives centered along the Columbia knew it as *Nch'i·wána* in the Sahaptin language spoken toward the south and *Swah-netk´-qhu* in the Salish language to the north. Mentioning old river places is likely to bring up feelings of loss. The river now covers homelands—ancestral villages, fisheries, and sacred places thousands of years in the making.

The Columbia River is alive and sacred to the river people; it is the place where the flowering of creation began. Among their elders are those who know specific places where the tule still grows and sturgeon live. Intimate relationships exist between various rocks and landforms, long associated with stories that teach important life lessons. Young children learn, for example, that the two spires below the Wenatchee River were Grizzly Bear and Black Bear, turned into stone by Coyote as punishment for their ceaseless bickering. It is like this up and down the river; each place holds its own story alive with meaning. These remembered places nourish the native people's connections with spiritual traditions stretching back to the time of the Ancients and, before them, the Animal People.

It is challenging to imagine rocks and rapids where none remain visible today. Even before the building of the great hydroelectric dams along the Columbia, many of its particular places were barely known. At the time, this gave rise to river explorer M.J. Lorraine titling his 1924 book *The Columbia Unveiled*.

If gaining a full sense of the river was difficult then, the job is even more so now, requiring something of an imaginative leap. Rivers do not lie flat on a page, of course, and their language transcends what our words can describe. How is it possible to do justice to a place that no longer can be seen, whose songs are now silent? How can one adequately put on paper something so living, vital, and surging—a river large enough to create hugely spectacular landscapes and sustain its sentient beings, be they fish, birds, insects, or mammals? Nothing substitutes for real life experience. Fortunately, those venturing to the free-flowing Hanford Reach or driving above Northport can still experience something of the Columbia's fast waters and old channels. The rest flows somewhere underneath reservoirs, to be seen only through the eyes of a previous generation that saw fit to record it.

Rivers appeal to all of the senses, not just the visual. My hope is that within these pages echoes of the Mid-Columbia's original music may yet be heard by imagining the sounds and rhythms of its rapids. The photographs and stories within these pages are designed to encourage you, the reader, to enter these riverplaces. Perhaps you might feel the wind close to the water's edge at Picture Rocks Bay, or catch a bit of the thrill and cold spray from running Grand Rapids with French Canadian voyageurs. The river has powerful stories to tell that embody a full spectrum of feeling. There's the eeriness of lining a steamboat up Entiat Rapids in the early morning fog with Captain Griggs, or the excitement of standing alongside Methow Rapids during the great flood of 1894, watching a rooster flapping its wings and crowing wildly while speeding downriver atop a floating haystack. There are stories of close calls, such as the unnamed Indian who escaped with his life after having fallen into Kettle Falls, or Captain Fred McDermott nearly losing his son off the deck of the *Yakima*. Other stories are tragic, such as Jesuit Priest Pierre DeSmet helplessly watching five boatmen drown at Whirlpool Rapids.

Native River is a book of invitation. Perhaps readers can enter an earlier world where it is possible to smell traces of smoke from David Thompson's pipe as he traded with villagers at the mouth of the Sanpoil River. Or one might wish to join Lt. C.E.S. Wood at Wenatchee Flats in 1879 as he watches the thrilling finish of an Indian horse race.

While working with this material, I have come to appreciate the different ways people hold memory. Immigrants to our region, both European and Asian, brought the longstanding practices of preserving their collective histories mostly through the written word. Indigenous people of North America retained memory differently—through their oral traditions. Remarkably, even today elders recall native names of submerged riverplaces. The spoken word remains critical to preserving essential lifeways that have been in the process of evolution for hundreds of years. Moreover, Native remembering involves more than speech alone. Shuwapsa, a Wanapum leader living at the dawn of the 19th century, spoke of this by reminding his people of the Creator's primary commandment: "Sing and dance that you may remember." Such memory is written in the heart where it is most deeply cherished.

The majority of stories are told from a European/American point of view. Where possible, I have included river stories told in the voice of resident Native Americans. For descendants of Salish- and Sahaptin-speaking river people, I hope that seeing these places frequented by your ancestors may add a measure of value to the continuity of your relationship with this river.

The fact that today we are looking at riverplaces divided into geographic and economic units is quite obvious when traveling on the Columbia. We visit Lake Roosevelt, Rufus Woods Lake, and Lake Entiat, all distinct entities. Yet even with our perceptions altered and obscured, we know that somewhere beneath these lakes the original river remains. The petroglyphs know it, the waters of its mountain ranges know it, and we know it, too. When I tell the Columbia's story and show old photographs of the river, there is immediate interest, as though a door opens.

Suddenly it is possible to *see* these important places thought gone forever. Curiosity and imagination spring to life, giving rise to expressions of wonderment. The sense of longing is made stronger with the knowledge that, through the means of photography, it is possible to see the river, though none of us can step through a door to the past and immerse our bodies in its waters.

At times I have been mystified by how strongly the Columbia has held my attention. Reading the text of a speech by Chester Keller helped clarify my understanding. In addressing a 1977 Columbia River symposium in Lewiston, Idaho, the Ellensburg philosopher made the following remarks:

> *Being residents of this Northwest basin means that these Columbia waters and land compose our bodies. Every hour, every day, the waters and food play through our cells. Just because we can walk and move around we tend to forget how literally the water and land reside in us and we in them…. The ebb and flow becomes at once organic and personal.*

In January 2001 seven bishops of the Roman Catholic Church issued a pastoral letter that takes our understanding of the river beyond the personal. They write that the waters of the Columbia are a revelation of God's presence, reflecting God's creativity in its topography, the diversity of creatures, and its ability to provide food and shelter to those who live within its watershed. Their letter identifies the Columbia as a commons shared by all members of the community of life. This underscores what native people have felt all along, that the Columbia's waters are sacred and need to be kept pure.

Philosophers of place remind us that we are engaged in an intricate and intimate bond with the landscapes we know. Tony Hiss, author of *The Experience of Place,* suggests that two things are happening at once in our ever-changing relationship to place. On one hand, we constantly scan our surroundings to locate separate objects that provide information, orientation, and stimulation, as well as protection, food, and other necessities for our well being and survival. Simultaneously, we are continually looking for ways in which we are connected to and part of our whole surroundings.

For those of us who live and work within the Columbia watershed, the river serves to connect us with our personal and collective histories. Sometimes we are conscious of the Columbia's role in our lives, and at other times the river quietly flows in the background. By learning its story, we come to a fresher understanding of our own.

Mouth of the Columbia   1

Beacon Rock   2

Celilo Falls   3

Priest Rapids   4

Rock Island Rapids   5

Kettle Falls   6

Dalles des Morts   7

Below Lake Windermere   8

Fairmont   9

Plates 1–9. *(See appendix for credits)*

The Columbia

Canadian ice fields and glaciers nourish the Columbia's first waters. Gathering strength from over 175 streams and rivers, the Columbia drains more than a quarter million square miles, and averages a steep, two-feet-per-mile drop along its 1,243-mile journey to the Pacific Ocean.

John Muir viewed the Columbia and its branches as a gigantic, rugged, broad-topped oak tree. Traveling north from Canal Flats in Canada, then reversing itself at the Great Bend, the river encounters and skirts around the vast basalt formations of the Columbia Basin. Beyond Priest Rapids and Hanford Reach, the Columbia is joined by the Snake River, whose additional volume empowered the river to carve a path through the Cascade Range. Flanked by majestic waterfalls and snow-capped mountains, the Lower Columbia passes through one of the world's most spectacular gorges. Massive and stately, the stream once known as "The Great River of the West" briefly flows north again before offering its fresh waters to the Pacific.

An enthusiastic though unidentified writer offers this lively description published in *Art Work of the Inland Empire* (1906):

Rising in inaccessible fastness, plunging impetuously up one side and then down another side of the Canadian Rockies, losing its furies for a time in the tranquil deeps of the Arrow Lakes, to emerge and battle again with basaltic barriers for many miles, now raging around the base of lofty mountains and then expanding into stately bays to pursue its ever changing but unfaltering course until it broadens like a sea to meet the tides of the Pacific,—throughout its whole course the Columbia is the grandest, the most impressive, most fascinating study of all the world's rivers, an epitome of the land which it has helped to make.

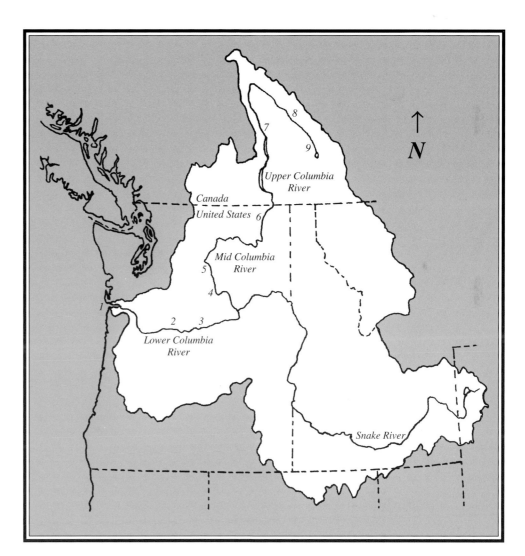

Numbers on the map reference photographs on page 6

Priest Rapids 10   Sentinel Gap 11   Lodgepole Rapids 12   Rock Island Rapids 13

Rocky Reach 14   Entiat Rapids 15   Methow Rapids 16   Okanogan River 17

Foster Creek Rapids 18   Long Rapids 19   Coulee Bend 20   Spokane River 21

Elbow Bend 22   Kettle Falls 23   Little Dalles 24   International Boundary 25

Plates 10-25. *(See appendix for credits)*

8

The Mid-Columbia

The middle section of the Columbia runs 421 miles between the International Boundary and the Snake River. In that distance the river once plummeted more than 945 feet in a series of about fifty rapids and one major waterfall, Kettle Falls.

From the International Boundary to its confluence with the Spokane River, the Columbia is lined by forested hills. Further downriver, the forests give way to shrub-steppe vegetation with trees only at higher elevations.

Throughout this distance, the river cuts through dramatic canyons. After meeting the Spokane River, the Columbia turns sharply west and sometimes even north around the thick lava formations of the Columbia Plateau. After turning south again, the river at Rock Island penetrates these basalts, and dark cliffs dominate the riverbanks through to Priest Rapids.

While hydroelectric dams under international agreements now regulate the flow of the river in Canada and the United States, two stretches of the Mid-Columbia remain wild. The first of these extends from the International Boundary down to Northport, a section of 11 miles. The second is the Hanford Reach below Priest Rapids.

Native River describes the Mid-Columbia between Priest Rapids and the International Boundary in four parts. Part I depicts the 59 miles from Priest Rapids to Rock Island Rapids. Part II follows the river upstream to the confluence of the Okanogan, a distance of 80 miles. Part III covers 109 miles, from the Okanogan to the Spokane River. Part IV continues upriver another 103 miles to the International Boundary.

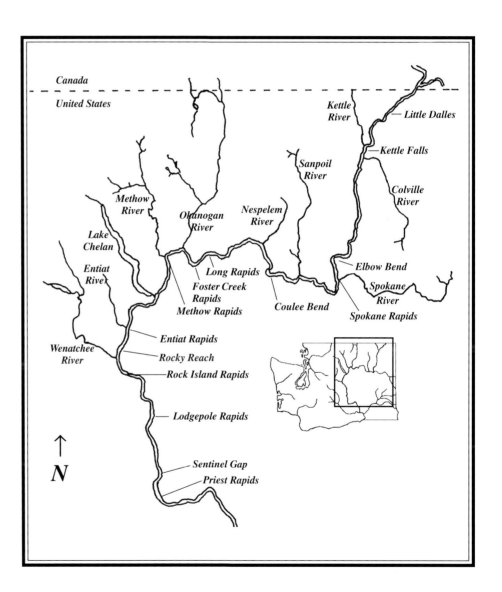

Plate 26. Puck Hyat Toot.
Click Relander Collection,
Yakima Regional Library

These images have been locked inside our lives for protection and safekeeping. They are not just images of scratching on stone. They represent those who have come before us and those who came before them.

Arlene Buck Miller

westerly spreading lava flows
stories of fiery arrival
taking millions of years
layer after layer slowed,
cooled and hardened into rock

along with enormous floods
carving these riverwalls
but a moment ago

precipitous cliffs
visited by men and women
with vision and song.

                    wdl

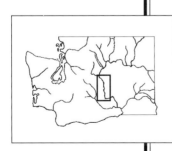

Plate 27. Priest Rapids, showing channel above second rapid, 1891. *National Archives (77HW 583-F-4)*

Plate 28. Birdseye view of Priest Rapids, from right bank looking upriver, 1891. *National Archives (77HW 585 F-3)*

Priest Rapids

Spanning 10 miles, Priest Rapids consisted of seven specific rapids: three at the base, two at its head, and two in between. The river here dropped 72 feet during low water and 63 feet when water was high. The fall of water at the lowest rapids was steepest, at 35 feet. The current averaged 7 miles-per-hour with some stretches attaining speeds of more than 12 miles-per-hour.

The Columbia at Priest Rapids ran through and over hard, rough, ragged basalt rock, yet some channels were quite deep. An 1885 survey measured the narrow channel seen in Plate 27 to be 60 feet deep. Known by fur traders as the "race track," it provided an exciting ride between two sizable islands.

In 1811, several Indians from a nearby village witnessed the fur trader-explorer, David Thompson, descending the lower rapids. Quickly, the Indians mounted their horses and met up with him a mile downriver, shouting, "Who are you? What are you?" After a brief meeting Thompson's small boat party proceeded. Forty-one days later, another fur trader, Alexander Ross of the Pacific Fur Company, met these same people as his party paddled its way north to the Okanogan River. He wrote, "Here a large concourse of Indians met us, and commenced the usual ceremony of smoking the pipe in peace: after which they passed the night in dancing and singing." The person leading the ceremony was a shaman, Ha-qui-laugh, for whom Priest Rapids is named.

Wanapums were familiar with the currents of these waters and skilled at paddling their dugout canoes through Priest Rapid's many hazards. In fact, on one occasion Wanapums left the heavier Hudson's Bay Company York boats in their wake as they raced one another down to the foot of the rapids. The York boats, packed with 2 tons of pelts and cargo, regularly sped through these waters, sometimes with tragic results. On May 28, 1828, three members of John Work's party drowned when a strong gust of wind carried them into a rock, breaking the boat in two.

Priest Rapids was carefully mapped in 1885 under the direction of surveyor J.C. Ensign. Indians had been asked to help with the survey, but declined, citing fears that such activity would harm their fishing grounds. Six years later, U.S. Army engineers ignited more than $2^1/2$ tons of dynamite in the rapids, but found that blasting the rock only created new hazards and obstructions in the river channel.

This locality is holy ground to the Wanapum Band of Priest Rapids, who regarded it as the place where the world emerged from darkness.

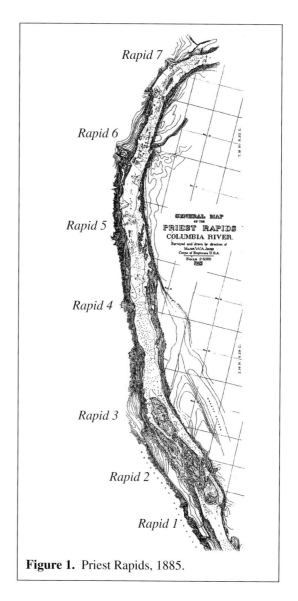

Figure 1. Priest Rapids, 1885.

Chalwash Chilni

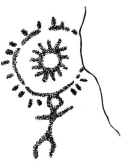

Plate 29. Detail of Priest Rapids, 1891.
National Archives (77HW 583 F-3)

*A*ccording to Wanapum teaching, the world has gone through three major epochs. In each instance, the Creator formed the world anew. This happened long before the Animal People roamed the land.

In one of these earlier epochs, two friends, Sun Man (Anhyi) and Abalone Man (Chalwash Chilni) lived on the islands at Priest Rapids. After a while a fight broke out between them over the use of fishing nets. Abalone Man, being the stronger, killed Sun Man who died with his head, arms, and legs outstretched upon the waters. The Creator was angry at seeing this and sent darkness upon the land.

Time passed. The Creator then made the Ancient People. He sent Sun Man to the sky and directed him to sit still, warm the earth, and watch his creation. There were no days and nights, no winter, and no hard times. The People had no worries about food. Perpetually bathed in light, the People lived in harmony. When villagers felt hunger, they sat in the longhouse and closed their eyes. Their leader would chant words of power, following which the People would open their eyes and find the finest of foods sitting before them. After eating, all closed their eyes again and the food disappeared.

One day their leader died. No one talked or sang the special songs, which, after a time, were forgotten. Soon darkness fell and the food no longer appeared. Huddled in their lodge with hunger in their bellies and fear in their hearts, the People discussed their plight. One of them finally spoke. He said they needed to remember the words that the Creator had given to their leader. Sitting together in the darkness, a man remembered a word from a song, then another. Line by line, phrase by phrase, the People recalled the words and songs until they could be sung

whole again. Listening, the Creator took pity, yet was angered at having been forgotten. He directed Sun Man to return, but only for half of each day. He told the People they would now have to work. To eat they would need to dig for roots, hunt for game, and fish for salmon. He instructed them to hold a feast of thanksgiving each year when the first roots appeared and the first fish swam upriver. The Creator then gave the people a commandment: "Dance and sing that you may remember."

If the People did this, the world would continue; if they forgot, the Creator would take Sun Man away for good and they all would be left to wander in cold and darkness with only lizards and frogs to eat. At that moment a new world began. One by one, every bird and animal, every root, berry, plant, and tree, emerged from its place of darkness into the light.

Adapted from Click Relander, *Drummers and Dreamers* (1956).

Although now under water, the island of *Chalwash Chilni* remains ever present to the Wanapums as their place of sacred origin.

Plate 30. Petroglyph on Chalwash Chilni, ca. 1955.
Bob and Ira Spring (#172929), Author's Collection

Priest Rapids Petroglyphs

*C*halwash Chilni over time came to be known as Whale Island because of a large granite boulder located toward the island's southern end. Elder Bobby Tomanawash remembers going to the island as a boy to procure goose eggs and fish. "We walked on the island with respect. We didn't sit or climb on the rocks. That's how sacred they were to us." The Wanapums told others that the petroglyphs had been made by the Mud People so that the First People would know about the nature of the country and its resources.

Most of the eighty petroglyph-bearing boulders were situated near the island's southern end, although single petroglyphs stood off by themselves throughout the island. Hammerstones, chisels, and sharp rocks were used to create the various figures and designs. Some figures showed evidence of repatination, suggesting that newer petroglyphs were imposed over older ones. As portions of the island were, at times, covered during spring freshets, 20th-century investigators believed that the action of water and sand may have significantly eroded a number of the original designs, particularly those facing upriver. Various boulders on the island held multiple images of human figures as well as mountain sheep, bear tracks, scenes of the hunt, and the rayed sun—all characteristic of well-known Plateau rock art traditions. Other boulders appeared to be inscribed with the highly stylized features associated with sites found more frequently downriver. Several boulders close to the water's edge showed serration, suggesting the possibility that the rocks had been used for sharpening fish spears. Another rock, quite different from the others, was entirely covered by deep grooves, suggesting the likeness of a mythological animal.

The Grant County Public Utility District's decision in 1957 to build Priest Rapids Dam meant the island would be flooded. After speaking with Wanapum elders, the PUD agreed to document the island's petroglyphs. Later that year, Arlie Ostling from the University of Washington catalogued each of the inscribed boulders, making muslin rubbings of them when possible. Smaller boulders were removed from the island, some of which are now displayed in a small park at the base of Priest Rapids Dam.

Wanapum cultural historian, Arlene Buck Miller, echoes the sentiments of her people: "They (the boulders) are a part of the collective memory that passes through each generation of Wanapum children, they represent a continuum of Indian people, of life, of the way our people live, close to our ancestors, our elders, our yesterday, and our tomorrow. They are a reminder to us of what is holy."

Opposite: **Figure 2.** Priest Rapids petroglyphs with map of Whale Island. *Grant County PUD*

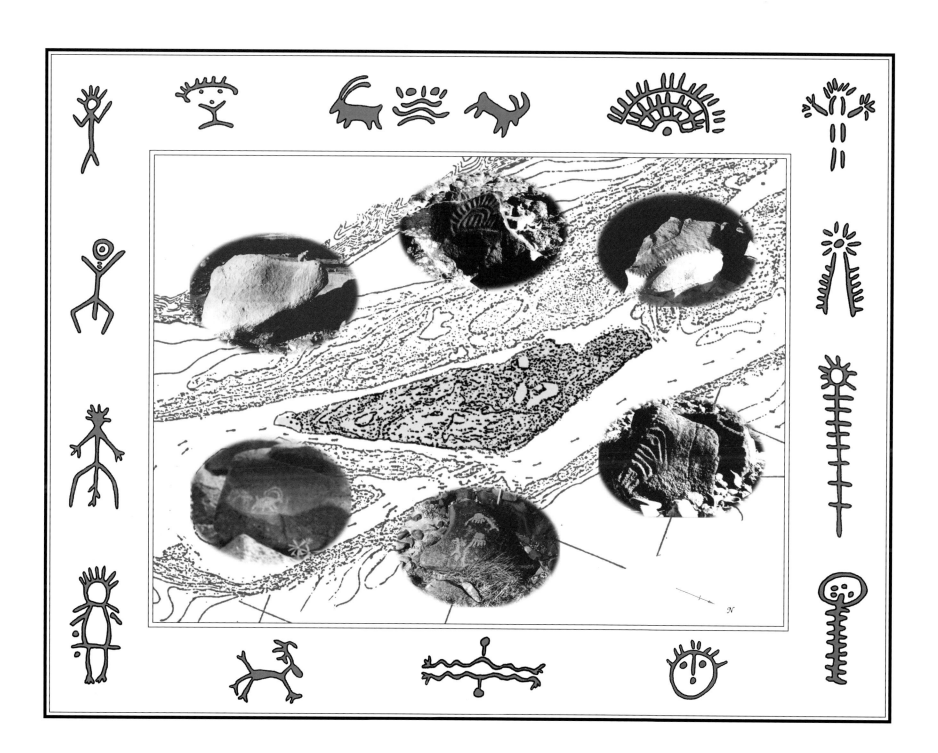

Plate 31. Wanapum Band of Priest Rapids, 1939.
Grant County PUD

P'na at Priest Rapids

Forlorn, barren, and sterile—these were words early explorers used to describe the arid desert landscape surrounding Priest Rapids. To the Wanapum Indians who lived there, however, this was a place of beauty filled with life.

Amid the never-ending sound of rushing water at the head of the third rapid stood the village of *P'na,* home to the Wanapums since life first emerged from the Sacred Island. Captain Eli Huggins of the U.S. Army visited the village in 1884 and noted that the largest lodge in the village served as the ceremonial center, with other dwellings clustered a short way upriver. A large fence of driftwood and whitewashed boards surrounded the village.

From the first outbreak of smallpox in about 1780 through the next century, times grew increasingly difficult and tumultuous for the Wanapums. Out of this period a *yantcha* (spiritual leader) arose. His birth name was Wak-wei ("arising from the dust of Mother Earth"), but later he became known as Smohalla ("dreamer"). Smohalla was said to have died several times. Each time when he returned from the other world, he shared his experiences with his people. He preached that they must keep their ancient ways. If they did so, a great transformation would occur where the dead would return to their bodies, the white men would die off, and the land would become rich with game and other foods.

In 1855 the Wanapums were invited, along with other Indian tribes, to meet with Washington Territorial Governor Isaac Stevens in the Walla Walla Valley to sign treaties. Known as a peaceful people, the Wanapums found little reason to attend the council. Instead, they chose to pick huckleberries in the mountains. Over the years, no one made an issue of having them move and the Wanapums continued living at their village. As late as 1939, large lodges composed of poles and tule reed mats sheltered them from rain, insulated and warmed them from the cold, and provided welcome ventilation and shade during intensely hot summer days.

Their traditional foods—salmon, roots, game, and berries—were central to Wanapum values and held in the highest esteem. Through the years, however, private ownership of nearby lands resulted in the erection of miles of barbed-wire fencing across the prairies, restricting the Wanapums from acquiring much of these foods. No longer could they travel freely to traditional root and hunting grounds. Fishing grew difficult as well, due to declining salmon runs. These restrictions culminated in 1937 when Washington State game agents descended on the village. With hardened hearts, the agents broke the Wanapum fishermen's gaffs and spears, and threatened to burn the village should they attempt to take salmon from the river.

This initiated a time of particular hardship. The only salmon the villagers could eat were those drifting downriver after having spawned and died in their natal waters. Word of the Wanapums' plight soon spread, attracting such allies as historian Lucullus McWhorter and State Representative G. Dowe McQuestern, who spoke on their behalf and worked to introduce a bill in the state legislature to authorize the Wanapums' right to fish. The bill passed in both the house and senate, but stalled when the state game commissioner vehemently spoke out to the governor against the measure. A letter campaign strongly favoring the Wanapum cause was initiated, but the matter was not decided until Governor Clarence Martin opened Item #12, a package containing the carcass of a salmon like those the river people were forced to eat. The bill was signed.

Despite hardship, the time-honored rhythms of village life remained. Each spring the river people convened to give thanks for the first roots and salmon, and to celebrate and acknowledge their way of life through song, worship, and dance. The practice continues among the Wanapums.

Sentinel Gap

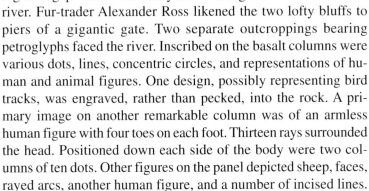

The Columbia cuts through a major basalt formation in the Saddle Mountains, resulting in a gap visible for many miles along the river. Fur-trader Alexander Ross likened the two lofty bluffs to piers of a gigantic gate. Two separate outcroppings bearing petroglyphs faced the river. Inscribed on the basalt columns were various dots, lines, concentric circles, and representations of human and animal figures. One design, possibly representing bird tracks, was engraved, rather than pecked, into the rock. A primary image on another remarkable column was of an armless human figure with four toes on each foot. Thirteen rays surrounded the head. Positioned down each side of the body were two columns of ten dots. Other figures on the panel depicted sheep, faces, rayed arcs, another human figure, and a number of incised lines.

A road built in the early 1930s cut through one of the groupings, destroying a number of petroglyphs. A larger road, constructed in 1956, demolished the remainder of the site before it was entirely submerged by the backwaters of Priest Rapids Dam.

Plate 32. Petroglyph panel at Sentinel Gap, ca. 1930. *Harold Simmer, Wenatchee Valley Museum and Cultural Center*

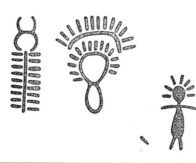
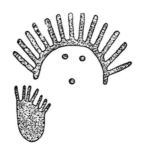
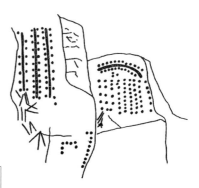

Plate 33. Sentinel Gap, ca. 1950.
Grant County PUD

Figure 3. Sentinel Gap petroglyphs.
Del Norquist, *Washington Archaeologist,* April 1958

Vantage Basalt Formations

Figure 4. Stratigraphy of Vantage and Sentinel Gap area.
Geological Society of America, March 1964

From 17 to 6 million years ago, huge orange-red fountains of lava originating from fissures up to 100 miles long in southeast Washington, northeast Oregon, and west central Idaho spewed huge amounts of molten lava across the Columbia Plateau. Over time, perhaps more than 270 separate flows spread swiftly throughout the region, eventually covering 64,000 square miles under nearly 43,000 cubic miles of basalt. Due to the accumulative weight of these successive basalt layers, and plate tectonic convergence and the uplifting of the Cascades, the central portion of the region warped downward, forming the Columbia Basin. Tectonic convergence also caused east-west folding, creating such features as the Saddle Mountains and Umtanum Ridge. More recently, from about 15,000 to 12,500 years ago, dozens of massive floods from Glacial Lake Missoula carved the great basalt cliffs we see along the Columbia today.

Each basalt flow carried its own signature, a unique combination of geo-chemical, magnetic, and physical characteristics. Some were less than 10 feet thick; others were hundreds of feet deep. Many retained a high degree of consistency over large areas, making it possible for geologists today to follow individual flows for miles across the landscape. Some flows spilled into shallow lakes that contained more than 30 kinds of trees, some of which had floated down from higher elevations. As lava poured into these areas, the waterlogged wood failed to burn and was covered up. Over time, silica and other minerals infiltrated the cell walls of the trees, hardening them into petrified wood.

Basalt outcroppings, rising up to 800 feet above the Columbia, are particularly evident from Beverly Gap to Vantage. Geologists have identified 15 primary basalt flows that form these cliffs. One of the earliest is dubbed "Confusion Flow" for the way it appears. Most of the flows are named after the localities along the river where geologists identified them.

Lava entering lakes and swamps generally formed pillow-palagonite deposits at the base of a flow, succeeded above by colonnades and columns and a vesicular crust. Of these, columnar basalt took the longest to cool. Frequently hexagonal in shape and often more than two feet in diameter, the smooth columnar surfaces were well suited for Native peoples to paint pictographs and carve petroglyphs. Basalt columns along this section of the river exhibited a profusion of images. Reservoir waters now cover them.

Plate 34. Vantage Bluffs, 1963.
Al Deane, Grant County PUD

river mile 422–423

Ginkgo Petrified Forest

The Origin of the Petrified Forest ~ Mary Summerlin

Coyote was walking along one day and visited Raccoon's camp below Rock Island Rapids. Seeing that Raccoon had seven beautiful daughters, Coyote approached Father Raccoon to discover if he might take one of them for his wife. The elder Raccoon refused because he needed all his daughters to bring in sagebrush for the family fire. Still wanting one of Raccoon's daughters, Coyote promised the elder Raccoon that in exchange for permission to marry one of his daughters he would supply Raccoon's family with all the firewood they might need. Raccoon then went to tell his daughters about the proposal, but none of them wanted any part of marrying homely Coyote. However, the sisters agreed they were very tired of gathering sagebrush and decided they would think on it through the night and before morning select one of them to go with Coyote. Before the night passed, however, Coyote, using his special powers, persuaded all of the seven to go with him.

The next morning a large pile of driftwood was found near Raccoon's camp. This so pleased Father Raccoon that he consented to let all the daughters go with Coyote. Soon the arrangement grew tiresome for the sisters. While they wanted to return home, the seven decided to stay longer with Coyote so as to make sure their family would have enough firewood to last a long time.

Coyote set about to work. He first made an eddy at Raccoon's camp to catch the wood coming downriver. He then went upstream, uprooted a large number of trees, and threw them in the river, where they floated downstream to Raccoon's place. To make sure there would be plenty of green wood when all the other wood was used up, Coyote also planted trees on the west bank of the river. After a time the sisters thought that since they had retrieved enough wood, they would tell Coyote they were homesick and wanted to return to their father's camp for a visit. When the sisters arrived at the camp, they were very happy to see the large piles of driftwood that had floated downriver as well as the forest of new trees. This provided assurance they would not have to carry sagebrush any more. After announcing to Coyote that they refused to accompany him any more, the sisters remained in their father's camp. Coyote proceeded to scold the sisters and secretly placed a special curse on the Raccoon family to take effect in three winters.

The first two winters were good for the Raccoon clan. They had ample firewood and held numerous salmon- and clam-bakes. The third year Coyote came around to tell Father Raccoon and his family about the curse he had placed upon them. He said the Raccoon clan would all die that winter and that in some future time people would come along and dig up their woodpile. Using his special powers, Coyote proceeded to change the new forest into rock and further caused heavy snows to fall throughout the winter. In spring, snows began to melt. Water rushed down the mountain, causing the Columbia to back up at Raccoon's large woodpile. The river soon overflowed its banks, burying the forest and its inhabitants in sand and rock. The trees still lay where Coyote sent the flood.

Adapted from Colville Confederated Tribes elder Mary Summerlin, who heard this story from her grandmother and passed it on to Ella Clark, who included it in her book, *Indian Legends of the Pacific Northwest* (University of California Press, 1953).

Opposite: **Plate 35.** Standing petrified log, genus *Lumbaramber* (sweetgum). *MSCUA, University of Washington Libraries, Lindsley 4633*

Vantage Pictographs and Petroglyphs

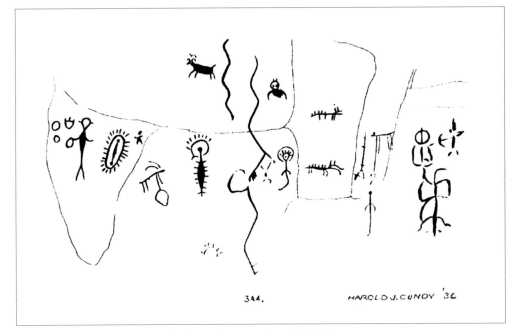

A cluster of four pictograph/petroglyph sites, now submerged beneath the backwaters of Wanapum Dam, stood close to the water's edge on Vantage basalt. Each outcrop possessed unique features. Two had fewer images and were located on small formations, while two others were of considerable size. Images that were carved or pecked into the rock predominated, but painted figures were found as well, particularly at the largest site, Picture Rocks Bay.

Early anthropologist James Teit wrote that young Indian men and women were sent to such sites for several days. There they prayed, fasted, and refused to sleep, all the while looking toward the moving water, listening for sounds, voices, counsel, and possible appearances of personal guardian spirits. Such extraordinary occurrences were considered highly personal and not to be shared, except perhaps considerably later in one's life. Taking a hammerstone, chisel, or paint, individuals gave expression to these moments of profound inspiration by recording the experience in stone, adding to the images recorded during previous quests.

Figure 5. Vantage I ~ petroglyph panel, approximately 10 feet across.
Harold Cundy drawing, 1936, Washington State Historical Society

26

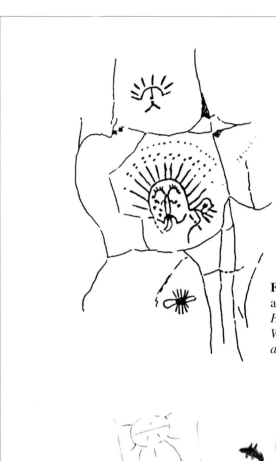

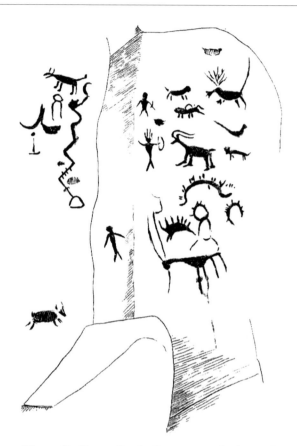

Figure 6. Vantage II ~ petroglyph, approximately 4 feet tall. *Harold Cundy drawing, 1936, Wenatchee Valley Museum and Cultural Center*

Figure 7. Picture Rocks Bay ~ petroglyph panel, approximately 5 feet tall. *Harold Cundy drawing, 1936, Wenatchee Valley Museum and Cultural Center*

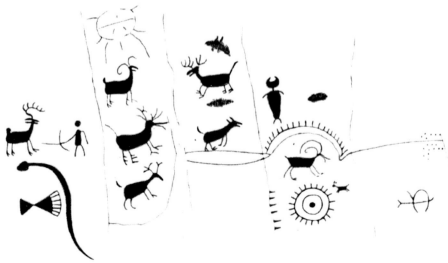

Figure 8. Picture Rocks Bay ~ petroglyph panel, approximately 5 feet across. *Harold Cundy drawing, 1936, Wenatchee Valley Museum and Cultural Center*

Plate 36. Vantage II, ca. 1963.
Al Deane, Grant County PUD

One pictograph and more than forty petroglyph groupings were found on the forty-one columns of this impressive basalt outcrop. Reachable only when the water was low or by canoe, as many as fifteen of the petroglyph groupings frequently were covered by the river. Others were located more than 10 feet above the base of the columns and could only have been reached by climbing. Several figures showed hunters with drawn bows. Other petroglyphs depicted sheep, elk, and deer. There were three sets of dual human figures, which anthropologists believe to be linked to the mythology of twins. Many of the images found here shared much in common with the Columbia Plateau style found throughout the

region, particularly the human figures with arcs and rays over their heads. Some petroglyphs were unique, such as one of a human form holding objects in its hands, with lines protruding from the figure's base and head. Prior to Wanapum Dam's construction, selected petroglyphs from this site were removed to an outdoor interpretive display at Ginkgo State Park. Upon viewing them, numerous visitors are dismayed that this remarkable site has been inundated. However, many resident American Indians take comfort in knowing that the remaining petroglyphs are well preserved under the cold waters of Wanapum Reservoir.

Vantage II

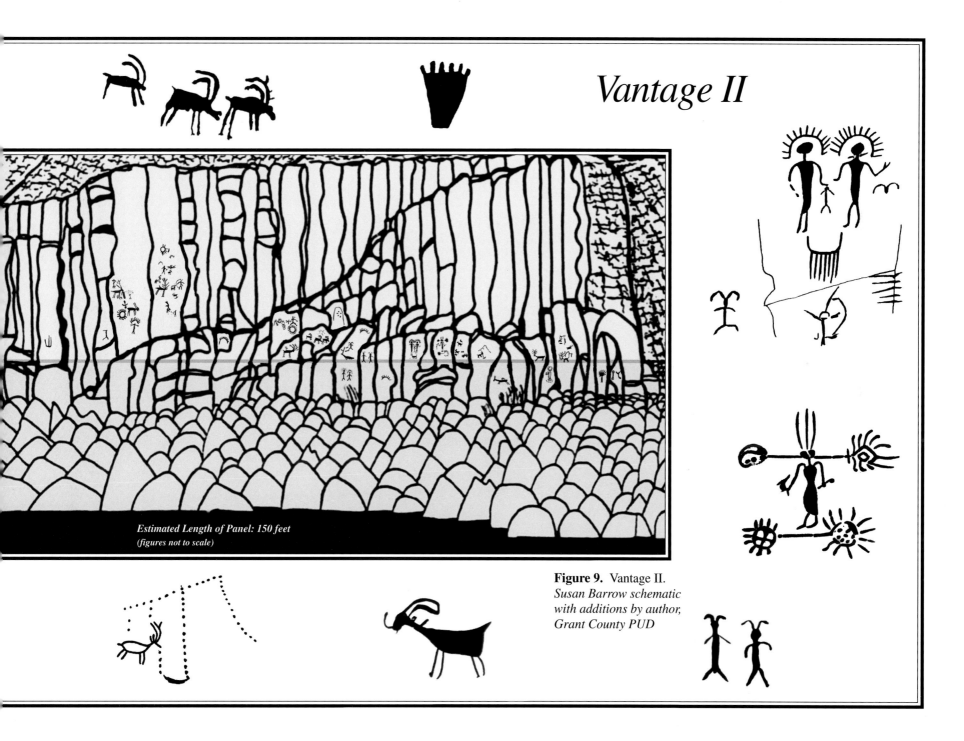

Estimated Length of Panel: 150 feet
(figures not to scale)

Figure 9. Vantage II.
*Susan Barrow schematic
with additions by author,
Grant County PUD*

31

Above: **Plate 38.** Picture Rocks Bay, ca. 1920. *Photographer unknown, Wenatchee Valley Museum and Cultural Center*

Plate 37. Aerial view of Vantage Bluffs, looking south. *U.S. Bureau of Reclamation*

Picture Rocks Bay

A visit to Picture Rocks Bay required either a rugged walk along the rock-strewn shoreline at low water, or traversing a narrow bench high above the waterline before the thin trail made a descent through loose talus slopes to the bay.

The place was impressive by any standard. Walking among massive hexagonal columns covered by more than 300 pecked and painted figures was a unique experience made all the more dramatic by the 500-foot cliffs rising from the shoreline. Both pictographs and petroglyphs were found in profusion along the columns of basalt. Quite a few were faded, probably by flood scouring. Some images stood apart, while others were massed in complex groupings. Some were lightly scratched upon the surface of the rock; others were more deeply carved. The individuals who carved or painted did so with a strong sense of style and feeling for how one element of a panel related to others. In several instances, figures were superimposed one upon another. In a particularly outstanding example, a white arced ray was painted over two red human figures whose hands were joined (see Figure 11, p. 36). Animals were drawn in all sorts of poses; some leaping, some running, some appeared to stand still. A few drawings depicted fantastic creatures; others represented known beings. Technique and content varied widely. Many of the figures were painted or pecked in geometric patterns and abstract designs, and some were expertly fitted to follow the contours and cracks of the rock. In common with other sites on the river, a great many figures included arcs and lines.

As with the previous site, several petroglyphs from Picture Rocks Bay have been removed and placed on display at Ginko State Park.

Plate 39. Picture Rocks Bay, 1963.
Al Deane, Grant County PUD

Figure 10. Picture Rocks Bay.
Schematic by Susan Barrow adapted by author, Grant County PUD

Picture Rocks Bay

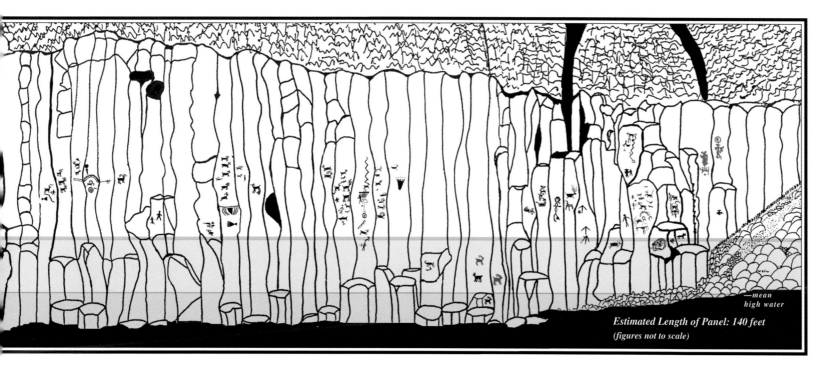

—mean
high water

Estimated Length of Panel: 140 feet
(figures not to scale)

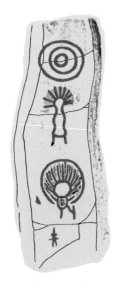

Pictograph
height: 4 feet

Pictograph
height: 5 feet

Painted petroglyph
height: 2.5 feet

Figure 11. Picture Rocks Bay.
*Harold Cundy, Wenatchee Valley
Museum and Cultural Center*

Plate 40. Pictographs and
petroglyphs at Picture Rocks Bay.
*O.H. Henderson, Wenatchee Valley
Museum and Cultural Center*

Plate 41. Petroglyph panel at Picture Rocks Bay.
*MSCUA, University of Washington Libraries,
Lindsley 4435*

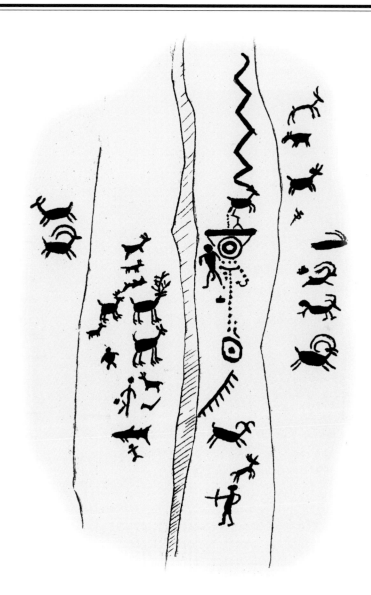

Figure 12. Picture Rocks Bay~
petroglyph panel, 5 feet tall.
*Harold Cundy drawing, Wenatchee
Valley Museum and Cultural Center*

Skookumchuck Canyon ~ Crescent Bar

Plate 42. Skookumchuck petroglyphs.
Wenatchee Valley Museum and Cultural Center

Figure 13. Crescent Bar ~ petroglyph panel.
Harold Cundy drawing, Washington State Historical Society

A short distance upriver from Skookumchuck Canyon, American Indians pecked sixty figures on a columnar basalt cliff close to the water's edge. Outstanding among the petroglyphs were four pairs of human-like figures similar to petroglyphs found at Vantage. Anthropologists indicate this may relate to a special significance that twins held within Plateau culture. Other images depicted an unusual insect-like figure and a human-like figure with snakes to its side.

The Crescent Bar petroglyph/pictograph site was situated at the base of a basalt cliff on the east bank of the Columbia. Figures were concentrated on two main panels, one of which contained more than twenty animals. In the above illustration a hunter seems to take aim at sheep. Situated on top of the hunter's head is a fish and above the fish, a human-like figure.

Plate 43. Spanish Castle petroglyphs.
Wenatchee Valley Museum and Cultural Center

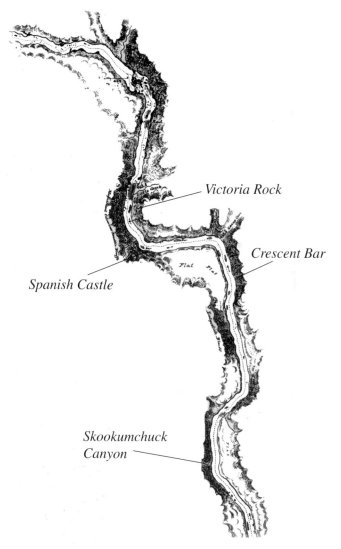

Victoria Rock

Crescent Bar

Spanish Castle

Skookumchuck
Canyon

Figure 14. Alfred Downing map, 1881.

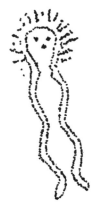

Between West Bar and the old Coffin brothers' ranch (later known as Spanish Castle), a figure with a body outlined by parallel lines stood at the base of another immense basalt cliff. As with about twenty-five percent of all anthropomorphic figures found along the Columbia, rays emanate from the head. Also carved into the rock were sheep, elk, five snakes, faces (again with rays), and several complex curvilinear designs. Backwaters of Wanapum Dam inundated each of these three sites.

Lt. Thomas Symons's Examination of the Upper Columbia River, 1881

Figure 15. Victoria Rock.
*Alfred Downing, Senate Executive Document, No. 186,
1st Session, 47th Congress*

When Lt. Thomas William Symons asked who might best be hired to guide a survey party downriver from Grand Rapids, settler John Rickey said that the only person who knew what lay ahead was old Pierre Agare. But the former Hudson's Bay Company boatman expressed reluctance to take the job due to his advancing age—he was nearing 70—and his failing eyesight. After several days of persuasion, Pierre agreed and soon Symons's party of seven was swiftly paddling the river current in a 30-foot bateau, the *Witchwater*. At the stern, Pierre guided the boat while Symons took notes from a perch on top of the baggage. Topographical assistant Alfred Downing sat on the bow constantly checking clock and compass as he sketched the river's course. After nine days, the expedition reached the mouth of the Snake River. Symons estimated

Plate 44. Victoria Rock, ca. 1920.
John Jay Browne Collection, Wenatchee
Valley Museum and Cultural Center

Plate 45. Victoria Rock, 2000.
William D. Layman

that they had traveled 350 miles, only 4 miles off the actual distance. His report described the Upper Columbia's numerous rapids and outlined the necessary work to make the river safe for steamboat navigation. In addition, the report included sections on the history, geology, and economic potential of the surrounding area. Downing's maps, drawn to a scale of 2 miles to the inch, show details of the river's topography, including the

location of settlements encountered along the way. Below Cabinet Rapids, Symons noticed a large rock in the middle of the channel in which he saw the likeness of Queen Victoria, her crown sporting an eagle's nest. Downing sketched the rock showing the eagle flying above the *Witchwater*. In the foreground, a snag floats downriver. To the right are precipitous cliffs, and in the distance, a grouping of tipis.

Plate 46. Bluff overlooking Buffalo Cave.
William D. Layman

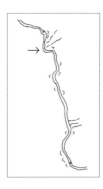

Remains of American bison have been found in at least thirty-two archaeological sites within the Columbia Basin area. One of the most significant of these was a kill site of eight bison in Moses Coulee, 25 miles east of the Columbia. Records from fur traders and ethnographers suggest that while not populous, a stray herd or individual bull at times wandered into the northern part of the basin up to the early 1800s. In spite of their small numbers, bison continued to be highly prized as a resource of food and clothing. Following the appearance of horses on the Columbia Plateau (ca. 1730), area hunters made the difficult journey east beyond the Rockies to find herds of bison. Buffalo Cave at the mouth of Moses Coulee attests to the significance of bison for people living along the river. A painted horse near the buffalo suggests that it was painted within the last few centuries.

Figure 16. Buffalo Cave pictographs.
Harold Cundy drawing, Wenatchee Valley Museum and Cultural Center

Buffalo Cave

How Kun-kun Drove the Buffalo out of Moses Coulee ~ Kikt-ton-nee's Account

In the long ago there were buffalo in Moses Coulee. Kun-kun, or Gray Squirrel, drove them out—

Gray Squirrel was a good hunter, small but very alert and courageous. He fell deeply in love with Morning Star, a beautiful daughter of a chief who lived on the prairie. Before approaching Morning Star's father for permission to marry her, Gray Squirrel returned to his own village for five days to hunt and purify himself. After leaving, another suitor visited the village and took a liking to Morning Star. He was the powerful Moos-Moos Si naz (Bull Buffalo). Impressed with his good looks and flowing black hair, Morning Star fell under his spell. Knowing that Gray Squirrel had planned to ask the chief for Morning Star's hand in marriage, Buffalo and Morning Star decided to elope from her father's village without telling anyone. When Gray Squirrel returned to the village, he learned of the runaway couple and took off in pursuit, tracking the pair to Buffalo's home in Moses Coulee. By this time, Buffalo's true character had revealed itself to Morning Star. Instead of a handsome bull, Moos-Moos was in actuality a monstrous, shaggy, smelly old chief who maintained tight control of his herd. Morning Star then understood that she had been bewitched. When Gray Squirrel found Buffalo's lodge, he quietly hid in a large yellow pine that stood close by. One particularly hot day, Buffalo took Morning Star to the base of the tree to escape the heat, whereupon the bull fell fast asleep. This gave Gray Squirrel opportunity. From his perch the squirrel shot Moos-Moos four times with poisoned arrows and a fifth with an arrowpoint heated in fire. Then Kun-kun called out to Buffalo and issued his challenge. Furious, the old bull got up, knocking down the trees from where he heard this voice of challenge. However, the four poisons soon took effect; the bull became groggy and fell to the ground. Gray Squirrel approached Moos-Moos Si naz one last time and shot him through the heart with his last arrow. Buffalo died. Seeing that their great leader had lost the battle, the other buffalo decided there was bad medicine at work in Moses Coulee and high-tailed it toward the sunrise. Morning Star came out from hiding and gladly returned to her village with Gray Squirrel. After purifying himself once again, Kun-kun successfully asked the chief for permission to marry his beautiful daughter.*

Adapted by Harold Cundy from a story recorded by historian Lucullus McWhorter, who learned it from Kikt-ton-nee in 1918.

Figure 17. Buffalo pictograph, Buffalo Cave.
Harold Cundy drawing, Wenatchee Valley Museum and Cultural Center

Figure 18. Squirrel pictograph, Rock Island Rapids.
Harold Cundy drawing, Wenatchee Valley Museum and Cultural Center

river mile 447

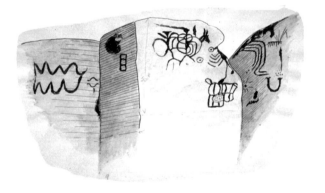

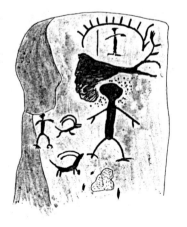

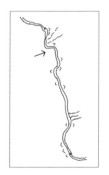

Plate 47. Cabinet Rapids, 1963.
Brian Holmes, Grant County PUD

Figure 19. Cabinet Rapids petroglyphs.
Harold Cundy drawings, ca. 1930,
Wenatchee Valley Museum and Cultural Center

River travelers encountered Cabinet Rapids, a noteworthy hazard, at a point 55 miles upriver from Priest Rapids. Situated at the foot of Moses Coulee, the water dropped 10 feet over a mile and a half distance. The mass of rocks appeared like a collection of tall islands, with narrow winding passages between them. Alexander Ross recounted the following experience here in 1811:

(August 22nd) We soon reached the foot of a very intricate and dangerous rapid, so full of rocks that at some little distance off the whole channel of the river, from side to side, seemed to be barred across, and the stream to be divided into narrow channels, whirlpools and eddies through which we had to pass. At the entrance of one of these channels a whirlpool caught one of the canoes, and after whirling her round and round several times, threw her out of the channel altogether into a chain of cascades, down which she went, sometimes the stem, sometimes stern foremost. In this critical manner she descended to the foot of the rapids, and at last stuck fast upon a rock, when, after much trouble and danger, we succeeded in throwing lines to the men, and ultimately got all safe to shore.

Nearly eight decades later, the noted Columbia steamboat Captain W.P. Gray lost control of the *City of Ellensburgh* in these rapids. The river current slammed the sternwheeler against the rocks, damaging its stern before Gray could safely get the vessel to shore.

Government engineers fared better in clearing a channel at Cabinet Rapids than they had at Priest Rapids because all the hazardous rocks were concentrated in one spot. Beginning work in April 1891, a work force of forty-three men drilled 472 two-inch holes and stuffed them with 11,000 pounds of dynamite. The last detonation of dynamite pulverized an obstacle 6,000 cubic yards in size. By the end of the year, engineer J.G. Holcombe reported that the channel had been cleared of over 12,000 cubic yards of rock. The engineers set ringbolts into rocks for steamboats lining up the river and departed, leaving debris from the blasts to be washed downriver during the next spring runoff.

Fur traders and government workers alike failed to make note of the petroglyphs at Cabinet Rapids. It is likely that many were destroyed during the early channel improvement work. Harold Cundy, an amateur archaeologist and member of the Columbia River Archaeological Society, visited the site in the early 1930s and drew many of its figures. In 1963 a University of Washington crew completed a survey of what remained.

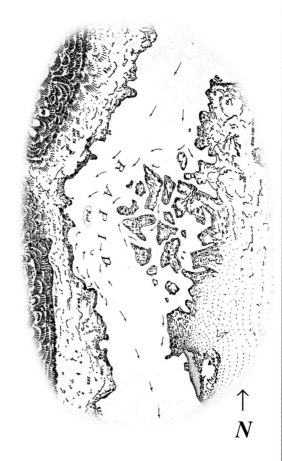

Figure 20. Cabinet Rapids.

Plate 48. Rock Island Rapids, ca. 1925
James Monosmith, Wenatchee Valley Museum and Cultural Center

Opposite: **Figure 21.** "Boat capsized here. Passing thro' Rapids on Keel of Boat."
Alfred Downing album, p. 31, Washington State Historical Society

Rock Island Rapids

At Rock Island Rapids, the river had cut into the dark Columbia basalts, creating two major channels around a large island. Over the length of the rapids, the river dropped 10 feet, slowly at first, but more steeply toward the foot where numerous rocks obstructed both channels. The sound of the rapids could be heard for miles, and within the narrow channels themselves the sound was an earthshaking rumble. For Indians, the many smaller islands, jutting points, and fast currents followed by back eddies made Rock Island Rapids a superb fishery.

For the daring, running the rapids promised exciting adventure. Hudson's Bay Company voyageurs were known to let passengers off at the head of the rapids before proceeding downriver. After stripping to lighten themselves in case of an emergency or accident, they pointed their heavy boats into the frothy waters with a rousing song. Lt. Robert Johnson of the 1847 Wilkes Expedition describes such a trip:

Shortly after starting in the morning we ran down the Isle de Pierres [Rock Island] Rapids. For about two miles the river rushed between lofty islets, against which the eddying waters foamed in their fury. The descent, of course, required all the skill and coolness of the bowsman and steersman; the vessel was tossed on the surging waters, with the surf and spray continually dashing over her bows; all at once as if by magic we were gliding along without a ripple on the surface.

Others fared less fortunately. Reverend Blanchet described a trip in November 1839 when the boat carrying his vestments struck a rock and broke up as it tumbled down a cascade. Worse yet was the plight of U.S. Army cartographer Alfred Downing. In 1880, Downing was accidentally set adrift at dusk in a small boat near Chelan Falls. Without a paddle and already having suffered from exposure to the sun, he helplessly rode the current fifty miles throughout the night. His boat capsized in the rough water of Rock Island Rapids just as dawn approached. For a time

he clung to the overturned keel, rolling over and over like a log. Realizing that it was to his peril to stay with the boat, Downing finally let go. He immediately was sucked under by a whirlpool. Struggling desperately, he fought his way to the surface and swam toward the rock-bound shore. There he encountered deep water, high cliffs, and loose rocks beneath his feet. Chilled to the bone and feeling more dead than alive, Downing finally crawled onto shore. Fortunately for him, several Indians who had spent the night spearing salmon witnessed the drama and came to his aid. They took him to their camp to recover. An artist as well as mapmaker, Downing later sketched the scene.

+ Boat capsized here
Passing thro' Rapids on keel of Boat

While mapping this section of the river with Lt. Symons in 1881, Downing probably recalled his trauma of the previous year. In 1888, the *City of Ellensburgh* became the first steamboat to ascend the rapids successfully. Despite efforts to make this section of the river navigable, commercial interests soon came to realize that taking a boat up Rock Island Rapids was entirely too risky.

Plate 49.   **Plate 50.**   **Plate 51.**   **Plate 52.**   **Plate 53.**   **Plate 54.**

Rock Island petroglyphs, 1930.
Harold Simmer, Wenatchee Valley Museum and Cultural Center

Plate 55. **Plate 56.** **Plate 57.**

Rock Island Petroglyphs

Plate 58. Rock Island Rapids, 1891.
Seattle District, U.S. Army Corps of Engineers

Rock Island could be reached only by boat or by swimming through the swift current at the head of the rapids, and piles of jagged rocks made walking there difficult. The island's abundant petroglyphs (with a few pictographs) were located in clusters, mostly on the northeast part of the island by the east channel. Amateur archaeologist Harold Cundy noted that the variety of subjects represented nearly equalled the number of petroglyphs themselves. He estimated there were between 350 and 500 different groupings of images on the island, some including as many as thirty elements.

The petroglyphs revealed a native world of vitality, animation, and story. Among the carved figures were elk, deer, sheep, goats, birds, bear, small mammals, a centipede, and a crawfish. Human figures abounded, some standing, others with hands raised. Some images appeared to depict supernatural beings. Several figures offered clues as to their age. Horses found on three separate rocks most likely were carved after 1730 when horses were introduced into the region. Other boulders suggest that natives may have used the island in a far earlier time. One showed a human figure throwing a spear, appearing much like an atlatl used to kill mastodons and other large game in a long-ago time. Other depictions found on the island showed men hunting with the bow and arrow, a weapon introduced some two thousand years ago. Not all figures were representational; many were of geometric and abstract designs. Two rather unique boulders stood apart from the others, one with deep pits and grooves, the other filled with cupules.

The petroglyphs reveal the fact that generations of indigenous people were deeply moved by their spiritual and psychic experiences on the island. Present-day Plateau Indians continue to regard these images as possessing great power.

Figure 22. Rock Island petroglyph.
Harold Cundy drawing, Wenatchee Valley Museum and Cultural Center

Plate 59. Rock Island petroglyphs, 1930.
Harold Simmer, Wenatchee Valley Museum and Cultural Center

Plate 60.
Rock Island petroglyphs, 1930.
Harold Simmer, Wenatchee Valley Museum and Cultural Center

Plate 61.

Plate 62.

In the 1920s, following several incidents of vandalism regarding Rock Island's petroglyphs, members of the Columbia River Archaeological Society erected signs along the roadway educating the public about their value. Society members briefly pressed for Rock Island's consideration as a national monument, but when rumors of building a dam across the island proved real, they quickly redirected their attention. Negotiating with Puget Sound Power and Light representative Les Coffin, the society secured an agreement to photograph the island's petroglyphs and remove twenty to thirty of them for safekeeping. Harold Simmer, a local Wenatchee professional photographer, documented 140 of the island's petroglyphs.

The salvaged petroglyphs, Simmer's photographs, and amateur archaeologist Harold Cundy's drawings, as well as photographs taken by Dr. Thomas Grosvenor in ca. 1925, testify to the extraordinary character of the indigenous people who frequented this place. The images reflect a time when animals were regarded as special beings, capable of imparting wisdom to humans in a life-transforming moment of vision and song.

Figure 23. Rock Island petroglyphs. *Harold Cundy drawing, Wenatchee Valley Museum and Cultural Center*

Plate 63.

Plate 64.

Plate 65.

Figure 24. Rock Island petroglyphs.
Harold Cundy drawings, ca. 1930,
Wenatchee Valley Museum and Cultural Center

Plate 66. Rock Island petroglyphs, ca. 1925.
Thomas Grosvenor Collection, Wenatchee
Valley Museum and Cultural Center

Plate 67. Rock Island petroglyphs, ca. 1925.
Thomas Grosvenor Collection, Wenatchee
Valley Museum and Cultural Center

Figure 25. Rock Island petroglyphs.
Harold Cundy drawings, ca. 1930.
Wenatchee Valley Museum and Cultural Center

Plate 68. Rock Island petroglyph, 1930.
Harold Simmer, Wenatchee Valley Museum
and Cultural Center

Plate 69. Rock Island petroglyph, ca. 1925.
Thomas Grosvenor Collection, Wenatchee
Valley Museum and Cultural Center

Once the salvaged petroglyphs were removed from Rock Island, the Columbia River Archaeology Society offered various suggestions for their display, such as incorporating them in the design of an electric fountain, placing them into the foundation of a new museum, or using them as a base for a bandstand. Fortunately, none of these plans materialized. For a period of time the petroglyphs stood behind a fence enclosing Great Northern Engine No. 1147 at Locomotive Park in Wenatchee. Finally in 1986, the North Central Washington Museum, in cooperation with the P'squosa (Wenatchi) and the Colville Confederated Tribes, moved the petroglyphs to an indoor exhibit at the museum dedicated to those who once lived and fished along this part of the Columbia. Four additional petroglyphs can be viewed at Rocky Reach Dam's Historical Gallery.

Simmer's close-up views and Cundy's drawings give no information about where the images were located on the island. However, a few photographs from other sources reveal that many petroglyphs were clustered upriver from Hawksbill Point along the east channel of the river.

Plate 70. View of the east channel from Rock Island, ca. 1925. *Nitschke, Russell Congdon Collection*

54

Plate 71. Aerial view of Rock Island, 1930. Arrow shows approximate site of petroglyphs on opposite page.
Brubaker, Seattle District, U.S. Army Corps of Engineers

river mile 453

Captain William P. Gray, 1888

In 1884, Captain William P. Gray made a reconnaissance of the Columbia River from the mouth of the Snake River to Rock Island Rapids. Based upon Gray's belief that Rock Island Rapids could be successfully negotiated by a steamer, a group of Ellensburg businessmen commissioned a Mississippi steamboat man, Captain Jones, to construct a boat and take it upriver to the Okanogan district. However, after returning from inspecting the rapids, Jones jumped on a train, never to be heard from again. The owners of the new sternwheeler approached Gray to do the job, saying that it was his initial report that had convinced them to build the boat in the first place. Gray wrote about his experience at Rock Island Rapids later in his life:

At the neglect of my own interests I agreed to take charge of their steamer, "The City of Ellensburgh," and demonstrate for them the rapids could be overcome. In July of 1888, we left Pasco with 45

tons of freight and several passengers on board for the Okanogan.... After sizing up the boat and its equipment, I didn't blame Captain Jones for disappearing. However, I had promised them to make the attempt, and I didn't intend to back out. You know they say, "A poor workman always quarrels with his tools," so I decided to do the best I could under the circumstances....

The only point at which Rock Island Rapids is really difficult or dangerous is at Hawksbill Point.... It required delicate calculation to overcome this difficulty. I put out three lines at the same time.... It took us two hours to pass Hawksbill Point. We had another cluster of reefs near the head of the island to pass. Here the current turns in strongly toward the bluff, 40 feet high, which projects from the mainland on the right hand side at an acute angle. We had no line long enough to fasten to the right

Plate 72. Rock Island Rapids, ca. 1920. Hawksbill Point is in the right foreground. *Wenatchee Valley Museum and Cultural Center*

56

point to take us across this bluff. The boat's power was insufficient to hold it in place let alone making headway across the current. The current drew the boat in at the head. We bucked the current for over an hour without success. I finally decided a desperate remedy must be taken. I took her across the current toward the island and swung almost against the island. It was necessary that I should let the stern wheel of the steamer go within four feet of the rocks and directly across them, to get out of the main strength of the current.

If the current here was too strong the boat would go on the rocks, break her wheel, and leave us disabled in the current. For a moment the boat hung where she was. It was a mighty anxious moment for me, for with all steam on, she seemed only able to hold her own. She was neither going forward nor back but slowly, inch by inch,

she pulled away from the rapids and out into the open river. That was the first time a steamboat had ever been through Rock Island Rapids.

The president of the company owning the boat was on board. His enthusiasm had ranged from fever heat to zero on most of the rapid. When I swung the boat over in the last effort, he wrung his hands and sobbed, "You'll wreck her, you'll wreck her sure!" But when we began to make headway and he was sure we were over Rock Island Rapids, he threw his arms around my neck and yelled, "You saved us—I knew you would!" Then I thought what a narrow line divides failure and success. Failure is "I told you so"; success is "I knew it!"

Fred Lockley, "Reminiscences of Captain William P. Gray," *Oregon Historical Quarterly,* Vol. XIV, No. 4.

Plate 73. Steamboat at Rock Island Rapids, ca. 1890.
Wenatchee Valley Museum and Cultural Center

river mile 453

Plate 74. Below Stemilt Creek, taken from right bank looking downriver, ca. 1922. *Harold Simmer, Wenatchee Valley Museum and Cultural Center*

Part II

the ancient riverbed
hits a barrier of basalt
and is forced west

east—the Columbia Basin
tall bluffs, little rainfall
west—ragged peaks frequented by mountain sheep
overlooking the river

between—a gorge of steep rock
terraces left by glaciers
at certain places the valley floor opens
providing space for lodges and places to hunt

flowing into the larger river are others
the Nespelem, Okanogan, Methow
Chelan, Entiat and Wenatchee
named for the people who dwelled
along these shores

wdl

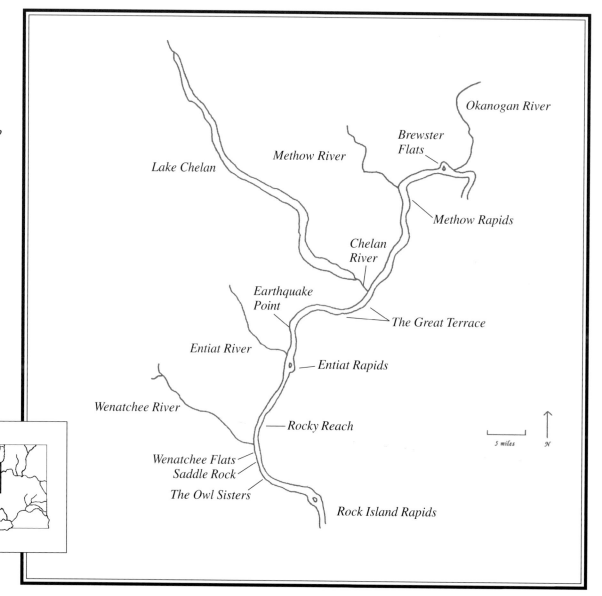

David Thompson Visits the Village of Kawa'xtctn (*Living by the Banks*), *1811*

Sunday, July 7th, 1811 ~ 8:30 A.M. *Soon after they depart Thompson views "high rocky mountains bending to the southward"—the Wenatchee Mountains. Beyond the Wenatchee River he spots a band of horsemen traveling south, but Thompson chooses not to stop. Ten miles farther downriver the current quickens and a decision is made to pull ashore. Here they spot two horsemen riding toward them from a village to the east. Thompson signals these sentries to approach the boat. Pipe in hand, he invites them to smoke. The meeting, however, is tense; no one from the village knows of Thompson's coming. The uneasy horsemen listen to a thirty-minute explanation of Thompson's journey and then hurry toward their village of eight hundred near the head of Rock Island rapids.*

By the time Thompson's boat nears the village, everyone has assembled in the main mat lodge, which Thompson judges to be 240 feet long by 30 feet wide. The boat is ordered ashore. Thompson again sends his Sanpoil interpreters to invite the natives for a smoke. Five village men emerge from the lodge to meet Thompson and his party and identify themselves as Sinkowarsin. They appear distressed and do not know what to make of these strange-looking visitors. Thompson, however, is experienced in such situations. He patiently explains the nature of the visit and, after a few rounds of the pipe, the natives feel more assured. Soon the entire village is signaled to gather round and take a full minute to settle themselves around Thompson's party. They are amazed to see men with beards and strange clothes. To the delight of the entire gathering, several of the French Canadians bring out their axes and give a display of chopping driftwood.

Even though Thompson's interpreter experiences difficulty with the Sinkowarsin dialect, the object of the voyage is once again explained and the natives' nervousness gives way to excitement and exultation. Placing presents of berries and roots before the explorer, the villagers begin blessing the voyageurs, clapping and extending their hands to the skies. When approached by any of Thompson's men, the natives quickly step back and suck in their breath, astonishment registering on their faces. A very old man moves to where the pipe is passed. After taking a few puffs, he speaks of how thankful he is to smoke this tobacco before he dies. Another man, positioned at Thompson's side, gently begins touching the explorer's legs and feet to learn if Thompson is like himself. "But (he) did not appear sure that I was so."

The visit continues for four and a half hours. Thompson observes that there are no weapons among them. The esteem Thompson holds for these natives is evident in his writings. The men are handsome, the women are very pretty with mild features, and the children are well formed and playful. He remarks, "Respect with kind attention to each other pervaded the whole." He notices that everyone appears in good health.

Despite repeated invitations to spend the night, Thompson draws the visit to a close. When the boat is launched, all the village members stretch their hands to heaven, wishing the voyageurs a good journey and safe return.

Adapted from William D. Layman, "Hawkbells: David Thompson in North Central Washington," *Columbia Magazine*, Winter 1991.

Opposite: **Plate 75.** Bishop Rock, left bank looking downriver, ca. 1925.
Thomas Grosvenor Collection, Wenatchee Valley Museum and Cultural Center

Bishop Rock

river mile 459

Above Stemilt Creek

The Owl Sisters and Sparrow Hawk ~ Celia Ann Dick

There were three Owl Sisters who lived on top of a hill below where the Wenatchee River joins the Columbia. One day the sisters decided to come down from their hill toward the river valley. There the Owl Sisters saw an encampment of many people. They thought that the people would be good to eat and proceeded down the hill to kill them.

From a distance Sparrow Hawk saw the Owl Sisters coming toward the camp. Sparrow Hawk did not want them to kill the people, so before the Owl Sisters could attack, Sparrow Hawk took to flight. He shot upward in the sky as far as he could go and flew down suddenly with the speed of lightning. He struck the owls again and again, piercing their bodies with his sharp beak. One of them died and toppled down toward the river. The other two were no match for Sparrow Hawk's ferocious attacks. Soon the bodies and heads of the Owls were filled with holes.

Coyote watched all that had happened and decided to turn the Owl Sisters into stone. He decreed that from henceforth, owls would be much smaller and would forever be harmless to people.

Adapted from story told by Celia Ann Dick,
used by permission of the Dick Family.

Plate 76. Sandstone spires on west side of the Columbia, ca. 1975. *Author's Collection*

Saddle Rock

Grizzly Bear and Black Bear ~ Celia Ann Dick

Saddle Rock is a well-known Wenatchee landmark formed from an ancient intrusion of volcanic magma. The Wenatchi-P'squosa Indians know the place as where Black Bear and Grizzly Bear once engaged in an eternal battle over their husband. The smaller rocks scattered to their sides are the bears' children.

Grizzly Bear was a disagreeable wife. She had a reputation of being grouchy and was prone to outbursts of anger. Black Bear, on the other hand, was hardworking and conscientious. She cooked good meals, took care of the children, and tended her duties at home. This earned her the respect of the husband the two bears shared in common. Grizzly Bear was very jealous of Black Bear.

One morning Black Bear needed to go dig some camas so she set out from the hills above the river to Badger Mountain. She rose early, took off her digging pouch and flung its belt across the river at Rock Island, forming a bridge that she could then cross. By the time Grizzly Bear finally caught up, Black Bear was on the other side with her belt back by her side. This made Grizzly Bear very mad and in a temper she tore up trees and brush before traveling downriver in search of another place to cross.

Once on Badger Mountain, Grizzly Bear neglected her digging by spending the day spying on Black Bear who went about her business of

Plate 77. Saddle Rock above Wenatchee, 1993.
William D. Layman

root digging. By day's end Black Bear's basket was filled with camas, but Grizzly had little to take home. Hurrying to get something in her basket, Grizzly broke what roots she dug. When Grizzly Bear arrived home to feed her husband, he would not eat because her camas was inferior.

Black Bear took care in digging her roots and upon returning home, she prepared them well. Their husband of course preferred Black Bear's camas. This infuriated Grizzly Bear all the more. Soon she even began having thoughts that Black

Bear must be more sexually attractive to her husband. Such thinking only made Grizzly Bear all the madder at Black Bear and the fighting continued.

As time went on, the two bears' quarreling got worse. One day Coyote grew tired of their ceaseless bickering and turned them into stone, which is where they stand today.

Adapted from story told by Celia Ann Dick, used by permission of the Dick Family.

river mile 465

Wenatchee Landing

Wenatchee residents regularly heard the shrill whistles and clanging bells of steamboats echoing through the valley from 1888 to 1914. A boat's arrival or departure brought excitement. Sternwheelers carried many things: loved ones to be joined, important news of the day, and eagerly awaited mail and freight—perhaps an organ, printing press, or cherished family heirloom from back east. Anticipation often was accompanied by a degree of apprehension, however, as the river had a reputation for unpredictable hazards—submerged reefs and rocks, fast currents, and dangerous rapids. Promotional literature did its best to offer reassurance, saying river trips were "animating but not dangerous. The passenger may recline in one of the deck chairs and restfully take in the ever-changing view." Things, of course, did not always work out that way. There often were substantial delays at the rapids along the way.

At 4:30 A.M. with a signal of the bell, one of the large paddlewheelers would back into the river's primary channel. Once in the current, the paddles reversed, with the captain positioning the rudder to steer the boat north from Wenatchee. If all went well, passengers arrived at Entiat Landing by 7:30 a.m., Chelan Falls by 11:00 a.m., and Brewster by 5:00 p.m. Pioneer journals recount that this was an experience of a lifetime. In the words of passenger Blossom Hanks, "there was something doing all the time"—the crew constantly shifting loads and tightening cables, the captain's ever-watchful gaze when threading a large vessel through narrow river channels, and passengers sitting down to sumptuous meals. Historian Lindley M. Hull spoke for many an old-timer in saying, "The people gloried in this transportation service, and those whose fortune it

Plate 79. Sternwheeler approaching Wenatchee Landing, ca. 1905. Wenatchee World

was to pass up and down the historical Columbia River will ever hold in grateful remembrance the resourcefulness and daring of these gallant river men."

Opposite: **Plate 78.** Looking north from Wenatchee Landing, 1897. *B.C. Collier,* Wenatchee World

river mile 465

Plate 80. Wenatchee Flats, ca. 1900.
MSCUA, University of Washington Libraries, UW 5519

Confluence of Wenatchee and Columbia Rivers

Alexander Ross, traveling north to the Okanogan for Astor's Pacific Fur Company in August 1811, found the Pisscows River (Wenatchee) to be a beautiful stream flowing from a low valley, skirted on each side by high hills. Here, he and David Stuart met the village chief, Sopa, who presented them with a gift of two horses. Stuart purchased four additional horses for a yard of printed fabric and two yards of gartering. The trade caused great commotion in the village, with natives quickly bringing more horses to sell. Stuart declined their offer, citing that six horses were all he needed.

At Sopa's invitation, the travelers spent the rest of the day at the village and watched several hunters successfully shoot deer from their steeds. Ceremonial dancing and singing lasted through the night, making sleep difficult, particularly when the dancers erupted in loud and deep shouts following periods of pause. The next morning the tired Astorians continued the journey upriver.

The Wenatchi village was known as both *Sĭnkŭchímuli* (mouth of river) and *Kultaktcín* (delta). As was true throughout the plateau, the population of the village fluctuated with the time of year. Its numbers always swelled when regional natives gathered in large councils prior to moving up the valley to the Wenatchapam fishery near the mouth of Icicle Creek.

During the first half of the 19th century, travel up the Wenatchee Valley by whites was rare, even though a steady stream of fur brigades proceeded up and down the Columbia en route to and from Fort Vancouver. In 1841, an American military officer, Lieutenant Robert Johnson of the Wilkes Expedition, observed Indians near the Wenatchee-Columbia confluence cultivating potatoes in carefully tended plots. In 1853, George McClellan of the U.S. Army visited the P'squosa (Wenatchi) tribe while surveying for a railroad route through the Cascades. Shortly thereafter, tensions increased dramatically between the whites and Indians throughout the Pacific Northwest, particularly following the Walla Walla treaty council in 1855. The P'squosa were required to cede vast tracts of land throughout their traditional territory. In a last-minute gesture to appease their leader, Tecolekun, a 6-square mile reserve at the Wenatchapam Fishery was included in the treaty.

Pressures on the Wenatchi escalated considerably in 1858 when news of a gold strike on the Fraser River resulted in a rush of miners traveling north through the Wenatchee country. In June of that year, one such group of seventy-five miners was attacked by Quil-ten-e-nock, a brother of the Columbia band's Chief Moses. Quil-ten-e-nock fell to a bullet while pursuing the retreating miners, but not before he and his party had inflicted several casualties. In the wake of the skirmish, military reprisals were carried out against Indians thought to be responsible for attacks.

The following years brought the first immigrants into the region. Two of the earliest, Jack Ingram and John McBride, operated a trading post near present-day Rock Island, but were driven away by federal government officials for peddling liquor to Indians. In 1871, Sam Miller and his two brothers set up a more permanent trading post just south of where the Wenatchee joins the Columbia. Their business probably picked up greatly in 1879 when General O.O. Howard met with a large gathering of tribes at the rivers' confluence. Soon, what began as a trickle of white immigration reached flood proportions. Within nine years steamboats were making regular upriver runs through the Columbia's rapids. Settlement was in full swing.

Yet, as late as 1890, a large council of 500 Indians gathered near the mouth of the Wenatchee from as far away as Canada and Nevada to air grievances against the U.S. government for its failure to live up to promises, including the one made to the Wenatchi at the council of 1855. Descendents of the Wenatchi continue to ask that the injustice of this unfulfilled treaty obligation be addressed.

An Indian Horse Race ~ C.E.S. Wood (U.S. Army), 1879

This bend of the river enclosed a level plain some mile or so broad, and just opposite the blue Wenatchee came from the mountain glens to join the Columbia. This plain was the council-ground. We arrived first and went into camp. The pack-mules luxuriated in good rolls in the sand, the canvas village arose, and very soon bacon and coffee led us to supper by the nose. Next morning our friends began to arrive. The news of our presence flew in that way mys-terious even to those who know the Indian's tire-less night and day riding and system of signal-ing. Hour after hour the Indians arrived, singly, by families, bands, and almost by tribes, troop-ing in with herds and loaded pack-animals, men, women, and children—for they brought their homes with them.

The tepees of buffalo-skin were put up, the smoke of many camp-fires arose and the hill-sides became dotted with grazing ponies.... The shy women in buckskin shirts and leggins (riding astride), their saddles hung with bags, strange utensils, and sometimes the papoose swinging in his swaddling cradle at the pommel; wild-eyed, elfin-haired, little bronze children, perched naked on top of some bales of household goods; the untamed, half-naked boys on their bare-backed horses, and galloping along in prema-ture dignity; the motley horde of patient pack-horses loaded out of sight under mats, robes, tepees, poles, pots, bows, spears, guns, and a thousand barbaric things of shape and color defying description. Last in the train came the grave, anxious-looking men in fur mantles or loose buckskin shirts,... their hair loose or braided, and their faces painted black, red, yel-low, white or whatever color pleased best....

Then the camp with its wild groupings, its color, its gorgeous setting in the evergreen and snow-clad hills... the irregular streets of dusky tepees; the lounging men, the playing children, the sneaking dogs, and the working women! There were on this ground the best horses of the whole Northwest.... The course was a straight stretch of about a mile along the half grass-grown plain between the camps and the foot of the mountain.

Figure 26. "On the Way to the Starting Point." *The Century Illustrated Monthly Magazine,* Vol. 33, November 1886.

The starting point was marked on the ground; the finishing point was determined by a horse-hair lariat stretched along the ground and held by two Indians, one from each of the competing tribes.

The finishing-point was nearest the camps, and here the horses took their stand, stark naked, save the fine buffalo-hair lariats knotted around their lower jaws. They were little beauties, clean cut as barbs, one a white and the other a gray; the skin fine, the sinews clean and silky, nostrils immense, heads small, bony, necks graceful, slim…. By each stood its rider, a young Indian boy, slim and sinewy as his horse….

The racers were examined again and again; hands were passed over their bodies a thousand times, it seemed to me. I believe there are no better horsemen in the world than our horse-Indians…. Presently, the owner of the white horse stepped out and threw to the ground a new saddle and a bundle of beaver and other pelts. Some one from the opposing side threw in a separate place a bundle of blankets…. It did not take long for the Indian excitement to grow, and soon the bets were showering down and the pile "swelling visibly" with such ra-pidity that it was marvelous how account could be kept. Blankets, furs, saddles, knives, traps, tobacco, beads, whips, and a hundred other things were staked.

Ponies were led apart in two groups, some wealthy Indians betting six and ten ponies at a time. The excitement grew to a fever. The men even tore the robes and belts from their persons and threw them as wagers. They whispered to boys, who hurried to camp and came up with new things.

The excitement, the surging crowds, the calling, the hurrying to and fro, the reckless shower of bets forming at last two piles five or six feet high and twenty in diameter…. When all the bets were laid, the riders vaulted to their places, and bending their knees, thrust them between the lariat and the horses' sides, thus drawing the lariat very tight and binding themselves like centaurs to their slippery steeds….

The racers now walked with long, supple strides down the course to the starting-point, accompanied by the starters, friends, admirers, jealous watchers, etc., some on foot and some on horseback. The whole mile of track soon became a lane hedged by groups and lines of Indians. The intentness, the care, and the suspense were catching. I began to feel a thrilling excitement and an impatience to know which of the beauties would win and which tribe beggared….

A faint cry at the other end of the line, a whirl of the horses, a tumult down there, a waving of whips, a wild yelling growing nearer, louder, and here they come—flying. Side by side, the naked riders plying the lash with every terrific bound; the Indians bordering the track packed to a dense mass, surging to and fro, yelling and throwing up their whips; the mounted ones running their horses at full speed after the flyers, but being rapidly left. Here they come! Heads out, eyes strained, nostrils stretched, forehoofs seemingly always in the air, the whip-throngs falling with quickening vigor. A horse, wild shouting, a deafening burst of yells, a swish in the air, an apparition before the eyes, a bound over the finish line, and the race is over, the white just half a length ahead, and there they go down toward the river, the boys pulling them in for dear life.

Excerpt from C.E.S. Wood, "An Indian Horse Race," *The Century Illustrated Monthly Magazine*, Vol. 33, November 1886.

Plate 81. Lincoln Rock, on the right bank at foot of Swakane Canyon, 1922.
Harold Simmer, Wenatchee Valley Museum and Cultural Center

The river canyon at Rocky Reach is 5,000 feet wide and bordered by hills rising 2,500 feet. Over time, the river carved its way down through the overlying basalt into biotite gneiss formations thought to be over 1.6 billion years old. Colorful bands of white quartz and granite metamorphic rock intrude through the ancient rust-colored cliffs and rocks.

A shallow, rocky reef extended out from the west bank, leaving a narrow, crooked channel close to the east side of the river. Steamboat travel through the 8 mile-an-hour rapids was manageable, but required a captain who could stay in the deeper channel and dodge the rocks that at certain times of the year were just beneath the surface. In 1895, government workers improved navigation by dredging the gravel bar along the west shore that formed the reef extending into the river. In addition, large boulders near the east bank were removed to allow steamers to take advantage of the slower currents on that side.

Explorer David Thompson spent the night of July 6, 1811, camped on the large terrace on the east bank of the river.

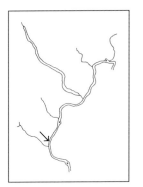

Opposite: **Plate 82.** Rocky Reach-Caribou Trail on the Columbia's west side.
Photo postcard, Ellis 384, Author's Collection

Ellis 384
CARIBOU TRAIL ALONG COLUMBIA RIVER

Entiat Rapids

Coyote and the Woman Wrestler ~ Bob Covington

Coyote heard of a woman wrestler that no one had ever been able to throw. "That's queer," he thought. "I have never known of a woman that couldn't be beaten by a man." Then he decided that he would challenge her. He was sure that he could throw her. He started for the place where she lived which was on the Columbia River a little below Entiat. On the way he met Fox and told him of his plans.

"Don't be foolish," Fox said to him. "You can never beat the woman." "Yes, I can," Coyote answered. "I'm going to try it." Fox still tried to persuade him not to go but Coyote insisted. "Oh, all right then," said Fox, "but first you go to that pile of rocks over there." He pointed to a spot nearby. "There you will find a pot of black stuff that I put there especially for you. Take that with you and you will be able to throw her. Before you meet her put down the pot and cover it up with your shirt. Then just as you are getting ready to wrestle with her say 'Oh! Wait a minute,' and rush over and get the pot and throw the stuff all around you and throw the pot down too. Then go ahead and wrestle and you will beat her." Then Fox went on.

Coyote went over to the rock pile and found the pot. It was full of a black, oily substance. He took it and went on up the river and met the woman wrestler, doing just as Fox had told him. Whenever this woman was challenged, no matter whether it was winter or summer, the river would freeze over just at that place with a very slick sheet of ice. Then she would always be able to throw her opponent because she could stand up on the ice, but no one else could. But when she got ready to wrestle with Coyote he threw the oily stuff all around and he was able to stand up easily, but the woman slipped and he threw her. Then Coyote said to her, "From this day on no woman will ever be able to beat a man."

Nowadays, when travelers are going down the Columbia River in canoes or boats, they always know when they are at the place where the wrestling match occurred, because although there are no rapids and the water seems perfectly smooth and calm ahead, the waters always boil up and turn over the boat just as it reaches that spot.

Told to Verne Ray by Bob Covington, July 1928,
from "San Poil Tales," *Journal of American Folklore.*

Opposite: **Plate 83.** Entiat Rapids, from right bank looking upriver, ca. 1922. *Lawrence D. Lindsley, Isenhart Collection, Wenatchee Valley Museum and Cultural Center*

river mile 483

Plate 84. Aerial view of Entiat Rapids, looking upriver toward Entiat, ca. 1955.
LaVerne LaDuc, Wenatchee Valley Museum and Cultural Center

Almost a mile long, Entiat Rapids was located at a widening of the river near the old town site of Orondo, about a mile below where the Entiat River joins the Columbia. Low gravel islands divided the river into three channels. Taking the east channel was the only practical way that steamboats could climb the rapids during the river's low water stages. The chute at the foot of the rapids was the most difficult, with captains needing to consider three challenging factors: a steep drop of roiling water, a fast 10.7 mile-per-hour current, and a sharp bend in the channel. Often captains needed to use a technique called lining. Stopping at the foot of the rapids, crewmen disembarked and, proceeding some distance ahead, attached one or more long, heavy ropes or cables to ringbolts permanently mounted in the bedrock or boulders. Then came the full power command and, with the

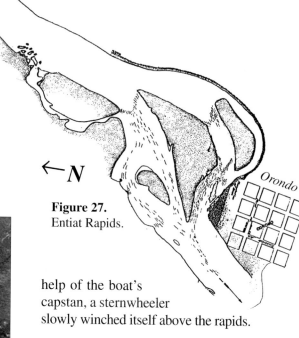

Figure 27.
Entiat Rapids.

help of the boat's capstan, a sternwheeler slowly winched itself above the rapids.

Fur traders had little difficulty descending the fast middle channel in shallow-draft York boats. When water levels ran high, steamboats also could take the middle or west channels (see plate 85). The rapids were notoriously dangerous and three sternwheelers—the *W.H. Pringle,* the *Camano,* and the *Alexander Griggs*—wrecked here in the early 1900s. If a boat lost power at the head of the rapids, it helplessly drifted into jagged rocks below.

Plate 85. Entiat Rapids, from right bank looking upriver.
John McClelland Jr. Collection

Plate 86. *Selkirk* lining up Entiat Rapids.
Wenatchee Valley Museum and Cultural Center

76

Dora Tibbits Casey, 1894

The scene beggared description. Just the first streaks of dawn coming over a desolate looking plateau to the east, the wheat-land of the "Big Bend" country. To the west, the frowning mountains, and ahead, jagged rocks, almost filling the river bed, some towering several times higher than the smoke stack of the boat, while around the submerged ones, the swollen waters of the Columbia made whirlpools only surpassed by those below Niagara Falls.

A certain fascination held the passengers in awed admiration of the scene, new to most of them. The crew, in the weird light of a cloudy dawn, silently going up the bank bearing the heavy twisting cable, the swirl of the waters around the sunken rocks, the mist from the foam encircling the deck, the call of waking birds from brush and tree, the meticulous care with which each act of captain and crew was performed, all served to create a feeling, not of fear, but certainly of apprehension, among the passengers. Something of the feeling that comes to passengers and crew, when all alone in mid-ocean, an iceberg looms through the fog.

A signal told when the cable was secured to the rocks. The donkey engine, as well as the propelling engine started. Two men were on shore, each holding a sharp axe with which to cut the ropes that held the boat stationary, as all the movement of loosing the boat and starting her upstream must be done at the same moment to insure a safe get-away. A slide backward, or a veering to one side of either bow or stern, meant piling up on the rough rocks around which the water foamed, and where the suction would carry down both wreck and people with small chance of escape.

The starting bell jingled in the engine room. The man at the winch bent to his work, and from the bridge rang the captain's voice, "Cut the lines." The man at the stern line severed the heavy rope with one blow. But the man at the forward line, confused in some never-to-be-explained way, failing to sense the danger, and clinging to his Old World habit of thrift, dropped the axe and started to untie the rope. This was impossibility, as with the rear end loose, the weight of the steamer caused the line to tighten the knots more firmly.

"Use the axe, cut the rope." And a vocabulary that river captains are always supposed to use, but which was not often heard from the lips of the dignified Captain Alexander Griggs, but to which one and all (even the Methodist minister, going up-river to officiate at a funeral) gave their approval, rolled from the bridge but with no effect on the stolid workman. The stern of the boat, now that only the bow was fastened, began to drift around in the stream, and was being rapidly carried by a near whirlpool, toward the rocks which all knew were only a few feet away.

"Take the wheel, Dad," and like a shot, a form sprang from wheel-house to deck, a second leap took him to shore, and before passengers and crew had time for another breath, the boat started forward, with her pilot, one of the captain's sons, standing, axe still in hand, over the severed rope. All breathed more freely now, and with the lessening of the tension which had held them, began to congratulate each other on their narrow escape.

Dora Tibbits Casey, "Reminiscences of a Ranch Woman," unpublished manuscript, 1930, Wenatchee Valley Museum and Cultural Center.

river mile 482

Plate 87. Entiat and Columbia rivers, ca. 1910.
C.M. Lockwood, Douglas County Museum

Opposite: **Plate 88.** Shil-hoh-saskt, ca. 1900.
B.C. Collier, Entiat Community
Historical Society

Confluence of Entiat and Columbia Rivers

The headwaters of the Entiat River flow out of glaciers 7,000 feet high in the Cascade Range. The river runs fast, clear, and cold for 42 miles until reaching the Columbia. A native village, *Ntià´tku* (weedy river), was located on the Entiat's north bank close to the Columbia. Lt. Thomas Symons saw the village in 1881 and observed Indians in dugout canoes spearing salmon in the nearby shallows. The leader of the village at that time was Shil-hoh-saskt, who early settlers knew as Silico Saska. They described him as a kind and dignified man, short and thick-set in stature. Gregarious and energetic, he thrived on the company of others and was well known throughout the area, in part because his village was located adjacent to Entiat's steamboat landing. Emma Meade, the first white woman to live in the Entiat watershed,

remembered her first encounter with Silico upon arriving at Orondo by wagon from Waterville. She and her physician-husband waited that evening for a steamboat to take them across the river. Enjoying the beauty of the Columbia in the evening light, the young woman wandered off by the shoreline. There she was startled to find an Indian in a bright red blanket standing upright in a log canoe as he paddled toward shore. After crossing the river the next day, she recognized Silico as being the same man she had seen the previous evening.

Silico and his wife Lam-a-i were fond of visiting Emma and her husband, Dr. Eugene Meade, in their modest log cabin a few miles up the Entiat. Conversations at first were awkward, marked by more silence than talk. In time, the Meades learned the Chinook jargon, a combination of native and English languages. Silico marveled at Dr. Meade's abilities as a physician. The relationship between their families grew through the years, embodying mutual respect and admiration.

Those who knew Silico Saska commented on his keen sense of humor. One day while ferrying Emma across the river, he spotted a large dead salmon decaying in the slack water near shore. He scooped the salmon's carcass into the canoe and laid it at the startled young woman's feet, highly amused at her immediate disgust. Emma asked him what he planned to do with such a repulsive thing. Silico replied: "By, by

dry it, mamomuc. By by four moon, ketchum snow, cultus tillicums stop nica house. Potlatch mamomuc." She translated this to mean, "when the next snows came, relatives whom Silico did not like would come to live off him. He would give them porridge made from this rotten fish and they would soon go away."

No one knew Silico Saska's exact age, but many thought him to be beyond ninety when the Entiat Valley was first settled by whites. He confided to Emma and Dr. Meade that when first seeing a white man, he had skulked in the bushes, caught between a desire to shoot the stranger with arrows and a fear of the consequences. He also told Emma about trading a pile of furs for his first shotgun, and of a runaway slave by the name of Antoine who planted corn on his land. Silico was angered at seeing his lands taken by the flood of new settlers. He told Emma, "Halo Siwash illihe. Boston man tenass illihe, tenass illihe, tenass illihe, tenass illihe [pointing with his finger north, east, south, and west], Halo Siwash illihe." Translated this meant "Silico has no land. Boston man take a little here, a little there, a little everywhere, till there isn't any left; no land for the Indians." (Many Northwest natives referred to Americans as "Bostons," because numerous Boston trading vessels had plied coastal waters in the 1790s and early 1800s.) Only after Silico became a citizen did the government give him clear title to 200 acres by the river. Years later he sold this property, now the town site of Entiat, for 2,500 gold dollars.

Ribbon Cliff

The Dog Whose Barking Drowned People ~ Michel Brooks and Celia Ann Dick

There is a hole in the bluff at Ribbon Cliff in which a blind dog lived. Every morning after sunrise the dog went on top of the bluff to spend the day. He had little sparrows there that warned him if anything approached.... When anyone canoed down the river, the sparrows would sing out, "Here comes some people down the river." The blind dog would then start barking. As soon as he barked, the water became choppy, tipping the boat over. Those in the boat would drown. Then the old dog would make his way back to the top of the bluff to rest while the sparrows resumed their watch. When more travelers appeared on the river, the same thing happened each time: the sparrows would sing out, the dog would bark, the boat would turn over and the people would drown. Clearly, the old dog did not want any people to go down the river.

The sun was angry at the blind dog because he was killing so many people. The sun thought, "If I do not destroy this old dog, then, when humans come to this place to live, he will kill them too." So the sun came down east of the river close to one of the sparrows. The sparrow
jumped up and made a little noise. The sun motioned for her to stay quiet. The sun said to the sparrow, "Don't make any more noise to warn the dog. If you do this, I will give you something to be proud of." At this moment the old dog woke up and said to the sparrow, "What's the matter that you made that one little noise and stopped?" The bird said, "I went to sleep and I was dreaming when I cried out like that."*

Suddenly, the sun appeared. Using his spear pole, he struck the blind dog's head, breaking it open. Bleeding, the dog ran up and down the bluff looking for its den. He finally found it and went inside and died. That was the end of people getting upset at this place. The sun took red, black, and yellow paint, and decorated the bird. The bird, whose name was "leek leek," looked at herself with admiration.

The ribbons crossing the cliff are trails of blood left by the old dog.

Adapted from stories told by Colville tribal elders Michel Brooks and Celia Ann Dick.

Ribbon Cliff also is known as Earthquake Point, where a strong earthquake struck on the night of December 14, 1872. Estimated at 7.2 on the Richter Scale, the quake caused a large section of the cliff to fall into the river, temporarily blocking its flow. One account of the event tells of an Indian woman who went for water at the confluence of the Wenatchee and Columbia rivers the following morning, only to find a dry channel! By the afternoon, the river broke through the temporary dam, sending a swell of water downstream.

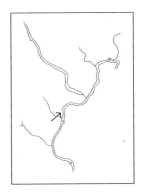

Opposite: **Plate 89.** Ribbon Cliff, right bank looking upriver, 1912.
MSCUA, University of Washington Libraries, Lindsley 3396

81

Knapps Hill

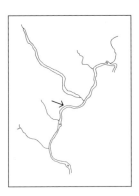

Plate 90. Knapps Hill, right bank looking upriver.
Lawrence D. Lindsley, Isenhart Collection, Wenatchee Valley Museum and Cultural Center

Near Chelan Falls, a series of terraces rises 200 feet on both sides of the Columbia. Known as the Great Terrace, they were created during the last period of continental glaciation around 15,500 to 12,500 years ago, when the Okanogan Lobe of the vast Cordilleran Ice Sheet advanced south out of Canada and down the Columbia's channel. Huge amounts of sand and gravel originating from farther north were carried

The Great Terrace

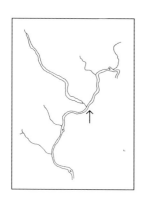

Plate 91. The Great Terrace, looking across at the Columbia-Chelan confluence, ca. 1900.
Wenatchee World

and deposited here between the glacial ice and valley walls. When the glacier withdrew, the deposits of sand and gravel remained in place. Eventually, the glacial lobe's retreat resulted in upriver ice dams break-ing and sending torrents of water down the Columbia's channel. How-ever, these floods were not of such magnitude as to totally remove the terraces, which remain today along both sides of the canyon.

river mile 502

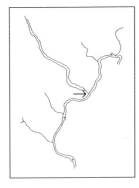

The Chelan River cascades down a wild, rocky gorge for four miles—it is the shortest river in Washington State. The drop of nearly 400 feet to the Columbia prevented salmon from migrating up to Lake Chelan. According to a local Indian legend, Coyote created these falls to keep salmon from going up to the lake because the chief here refused to give his daughters away.

A native village, *Sxa´tqu* (water pouring out), stood near where the Chelan River joins the Columbia. Chelan natives climbed trails from the river up to the 50-mile-long lake that extends into the heart of the Cascade Range. In 1880, the U.S. Army built a wagon road to carry supplies up the hill to a new fort on the lake. Fort Chelan was abandoned after a year. However, the steep wagon road soon was being used by immigrants passing through the small settlement of Chelan Falls on the Columbia and proceeding to a newly established town site at the foot of the lake.

Following 1860, Chinese miners established a village on the left bank of the Columbia about a mile north of the Chelan River. The store located here was known to carry one of the largest stock of items in the region. Each year, Wapato John, a Chelan Indian, led the shopowner's string of pack mules east to Ritzville to obtain merchandise for the store.

At one time there may have been as many as 300 Chinese working the gravel beds for gold at Chelan Falls. Their population was reduced in 1875 when an alleged group of Indians massacred a large number of them. Newspapers reported that the attackers struck quickly, trapping their victims against a cliff and then throwing them into the river. Recently it has come to light that the newspapers may have been in error. Early settler James Pattie told descendants that he knew a Chinese storekeeper, Que Yu, who arrived in the Chelan Falls vicinity several years after the attack. Que Yu told him that the story circulating among the Chinese indicated the atrocity was actually committed by white miners dressed as Indians.

Plate 92. Que Yu, Chinese storekeeper at Chelan Falls.
Marjorie Pattie McGrath Collection

Opposite: **Plate 93.** View of Chelan-Columbia confluence, taken from right bank looking upriver, ca. 1907.
Wenatchee Valley Museum and Cultural Center

Confluence of Chelan and Columbia Rivers

river mile 503

about 10 feet wide

Figure 28. Pictograph panel at Azwell.
Harold Cundy drawing, Wenatchee Valley Museum and Cultural Center

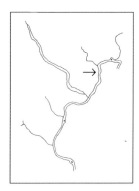

While rock carvings predominated on sites downriver from Rock Island Rapids, Native Americans north of the Wenatchee River generally preferred painting figurines on dense granite rock surfaces. One of these sites was located near the present Chelan-Okanogan county boundary. A variety of figures were painted on the granite overhang, including a rattlesnake, humans with digits on hands and feet, three circles with an intersecting line, rayed arcs, and an image that early rock art investigator Harold Cundy thought was scorpions copulating. In 1964, the Douglas County Public Utility District moved the large rock panel to a small park above Wells Dam.

Opposite: **Plate 94.** Looking downriver toward former pictograph site, 1997. *William D. Layman*

Figure 29.
Methow Rapids.

Plate 95. Methow Rapids, left bank looking downriver, ca. 1960.
Author's Collection

Methow Rapids

In July 1811, David Thompson observed Indians spearing salmon from these rocks.

The protruding rocks constricted the Columbia's flow to a narrow, deep channel. At low water the rapids were mild with only a slight drop. When the river was high, the water fell in excess of five feet, forming rollers and dangerous whirlpools. Early pioneer Nellie Gallarno recalled the great flood of 1894:

During high water almost anything could be seen floating down the Columbia, entire buildings, haystacks, wagons, beds, boats, barrels and numerous other things. One morning a haystack floated past with a rooster standing on its highest point, flapping his wings and crowing. To our surprise it went through the rapids intact, the rooster still crowing.

Sternwheelers had no difficulty ascending the rapids in low water, but needed a full head of steam when the river ran high. Oldtimer Ted Borg fondly remembered that as a boy, he and his friends often heard the whistle of a steamboat in the rapids. Immediately, they ran to a place along the riverbank that they called "the corner" and watched boats struggling up the rapids. Occasionally a line used for winching a boat broke, sending a sternwheeler spiraling downriver.

While affording amusement and excitement to some, the rapids brought grief to others. In May 1895, river surveyor C.F.B. Haskell, his best friend's wife, Mrs. Prowell, and deckhand Billy Barton transferred from the *Ellensburgh* to a small rowboat in order to reach the government skiff being used for the survey. The rowboat quickly was caught in the flood-stage current and headed directly into a whirlpool that spun the helpless boat around and around. Passengers on the steamboat watched in horror as, in a manner of moments, the rowboat tipped upward and disappeared altogether. Newspapers reported that Haskell's body never was recovered, citing an old saying that the Columbia never gave up its dead.

In 1894 and 1907, government engineers took out the most dangerous rocks jutting from the shoreline. Newspapers reported that a dynamite charge set off in the spring of 1907 broke all of the windows in Pateros, located a mile upriver.

Methow Rapids was situated a short distance downriver from where the Methow River joins the Columbia. The east shore was irregular, broken by high rock ledges jutting far out in the channel. The Methow band called the place *Xantici·'n* (little rocky gate). Small inlets behind protruding rocks created back eddies where salmon rested before proceeding upriver.

Plate 96. Methow Rapids, left bank looking across river, ca. 1960.
Author's Collection

river mile 523

Struggles in Ascending Methow Rapids

At times, the lining of sternwheelers up the rapids did not go as planned, as the well-known western novelist Owen Wister noted during an 1898 trip:

The captain wore a grizzled, unmitigated beard, more violent even than his occasional language.... The rapids below Pateros, where the Methow flows into the Columbia...it appeared, were more energetic than their predecessors.... The boat panted and shook, and we climbed slowly by the help of the straining rope to near the head of those rapids, when the rope parted with a wild cavort, and the boat went backward down the river, while the captain dashed his hat on the deck and danced on it all the way, swearing at every leap.... At the foot of the rapids we came to a halt. The plank was again lifted ashore...the dry land looked very good to me. (Guy Waring, *My Pioneer Past,* 1936)

Frank Albertson left this 1903 account of another failed attempt:

Power was applied to the paddlewheel in back and the capstan in front. There was no way to guide the boat. We were told to stand in front to hold the front end down. We were near the ring bolt when a log came down fast, hitting the port side of the bow. The boat shot out to the middle of the river. They signaled to cut the line loose and away we went spinning around like a top. We thought we were gone. The boat went about a mile downstream before it was controlled. The captain brought the North Star *back as far as he could and tied up. Harve, who had worked on Puget Sound boats for 18 months, told the captain what he thought of this procedure.* (*Okanogan County Heritage,* June 1966)

Some boats even failed to make it as far as Methow Rapids. John Weber's daughter recalled the following incident:

That day in May in 1906 when Dad Weber boarded the Selkirk *in Wenatchee to make the trip to locate the land for his homestead, he expected to land at Brewster that evening. But the river was roaring high.... As dusk settled, they had just made it to the Pateros [Methow] Rapids.... The captain wisely decided not to try to run it in the gathering darkness.... The passengers were served an evening meal and bedded down for the night. Weber awoke several hours later to hear as well as feel the bump-bump-bump of the boat against the rocks. He thought the night watchman had let some lines get loose and that the poles had dropped out of position, thus letting the current push them into shallow water. All at once he heard a terrific ruckus on deck. Running feet and roaring men made a commotion too interesting to ignore. Grabbing his pants and his derby hat he headed for the deck, hoping to see a good bare-knuckle fight. Instead, there was the captain cussing out the night watchman with all the vernacular he had accumulated while the crew was taking from the galley lard, bacon slabs, and anything else they could find to make a quick, hot fire. Weber glanced at the shore. Entiat was just coming into view! He was almost back to where he had started the day before. The desperate crew managed to work up a head of steam just in time to make the landing at Entiat. And so began the third traversal of the one-way ticket's distance. That night he docked at Brewster and caught the stage for Bridgeport to begin a new life in a new land.* (*Okanogan County Heritage,* March 1965)

Opposite: **Plate 97.** *Okanogan ascending Methow Rapids.*
Lee Cooper Family

river mile 523

Confluence of Methow and Columbia Rivers

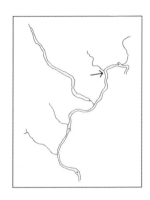

Plate 98. Ives Landing, from Billy Goat Mountain, ca. 1900. *George Wilson Collection*

The Methow River begins high in the North Cascades and flows 69 miles to join the Columbia at Pateros. Large quantities of sand and sediment at the river's outlet formed a bar where first white, and then Chinese, miners sluiced for gold between about 1860 and 1900. When Lee Ives settled here in 1886, he noted an Indian village of twenty tipis as well as numerous Chinese dugout huts. Much earlier, both David Thompson and Alexander Ross stopped at an Indian village at the confluence of these rivers. Their respective journal entries indicate that they were received warmly by the villagers living here. In all likelihood, news of their coming already had arrived by Indian messengers before the explorers disembarked from their boats.

Brewster Riffle

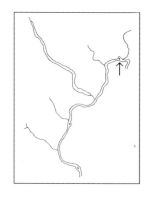

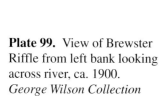

Plate 99. View of Brewster Riffle from left bank looking across river, ca. 1900. *George Wilson Collection*

Near the old town site of Virginia City (located just below Brewster), the Columbia temporarily turned to the north. Here the river skirted around large gravel bars formed when yearly spring freshets unloaded thousands of tons of sand and gravel into the Columbia. Covering a two-square-mile area near the mouth of the Okanogan River, these probably were the gravel bars that early placer miners called Rich Bar. U.E. Fries, author of *From Copenhagen to Okanogan*, heard stories about prospectors taking out $100,000 in gold from this section of river. Chinese miners soon followed, reworking claims left by white miners who had moved on in search of bigger strikes.

U.E. Fries, 1898

*O*ne day Pete [McPherson] had taken the ferry across to the Douglas County side to bring over a four-horse team, a loaded wagon, and a man and his wife. Going over, there was no trouble but on the return trip, before they had reached the middle of the stream and just where the current was extremely swift, a drifting log struck the ferry on the bow end. Pete, having seen the danger coming, braced himself and held on firmly to the windlass, but the impact was so terrific that he was thrown over the wheel head first into the river. The swift current took him under the boat, but he swam out and managed to reach the Douglas County shore.

As the ferry was now left without guidance, the bow end of the boat no longer pointed upstream, and the current struck her broadside. The resultant strain was so terrific that the two-inch rope holding the boat to the cable gave way. Down stream went the ferry with its load and passengers, headed for the dangerous Methow Rapids six miles below.

McCarter, the blacksmith, had been watching the crossing because of the danger threatened by the increased speed of the current and by the occasional drift. Then, seeing what had happened to the ferry, he turned to give the alarm. Just as he did so, Captain Alexander Griggs came in sight, returning from a trip to Conconully with McCarter's livery team and buggy. He called out, "Captain, the ferryboat has just broken loose in the middle of the river and is drifting away— and Pete McPherson is in the river."

Without answering a word, the captain whipped up his horses, headed them down the river, and left the town as though he were driving a pair of runaways.

Meanwhile the man on the ferry got into the light rowboat, which was kept tied alongside for emergency use. He had had no experience in the water and started to row upstream. Central Ferry came in sight, but the runaway boat passed right under its cable on the way downstream. The Central ferryman hurriedly jumped into his little rowboat and caught up with the ferry midstream. He tied onto the end nearest him, but now the two men in rowboats were rowing against each other, and the current was having its way with them.

Captain Griggs, driving along the Okanogan bank, soon overtook them and yelled instructions as to what to do. At first they did not understand him, but, finally, doing as he said, and attaching both boats to the Okanogan end of the ferryboat, they succeeded in landing it a couple of miles above Pateros. There it remained until the river dropped and all the drift had gone on downstream. Then Captain Griggs fastened the ferry alongside his *City of Ellensburgh* and towed it home to Virginia City.

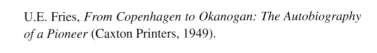

U.E. Fries, *From Copenhagen to Okanogan: The Autobiography of a Pioneer* (Caxton Printers, 1949).

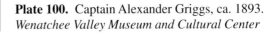

Plate 100. Captain Alexander Griggs, ca. 1893.
Wenatchee Valley Museum and Cultural Center

Plate 101. Early Brewster.
Mikel, Wenatchee World

How Mountain Goat Won Coyote's Daughter ~ Peter Wapato

Coyote used to live right here on Brewster Flat. He had a most beautiful daughter who could run faster than any animal living. Many a young man wanted her for his wife, but Coyote was determined that she should remain unmarried, so that she might keep house for him in his old age. Despite her father's determination that she remain single, the girl was beset by suitors.

Now Coyote was shrewd and thoroughly unscrupulous. After some reflection on the matter, he contrived a way to keep his daughter unmarried throughout his lifetime, a way which would capitalize on the infatuation of the young men as well. He promised to give his daughter in marriage to anyone who should beat her in a foot race, but if a young man lost the race, he must forfeit all his earthly possessions, and his life to boot!

Coyote's scheme succeeded very well, indeed. The more ardent suitors were soon eliminated, and Coyote became immensely wealthy with blankets, pelts, knives, ornaments, and the like, which became his property when the young men lost the race and their lives as well. After a while no one would risk his life in the vain attempt to win Coyote's daughter, and it seemed as if the girl was doomed to spinsterhood.

At this juncture, however, a new and immensely wealthy suitor appeared on the scene. He was Mountain Goat who lived high amid the snow peaks at the head of Lake Chelan. He saw Coyote's daughter and fell deeply in love with her. When he saw that the Goat was attracted by the girl, Coyote was overjoyed, because Mountain Goat had great possessions and the cunning Coyote had no doubt that they would soon become his own.

The terms of the race did not deter the love-smitten Goat. The day for the race was set. Mountain Goat returned to his home at the head of the lake where he engaged two nimble little spike horn bucks to run the race for him, with the provision that if they won the race, the Goat was to take the girl for his wife. Then he brewed up a great, great, strong medicine. The night before the contest he returned to Brewster Flat where he sprinkled the strong medicine all along the course where the race was to be run.

The day for the contest arrived. Coyote's daughter realized that to win the race she must run faster than she ever had run before. She took off her moccasins to run in her bare feet. The starting signal was given. Coyote's daughter shot out into the lead and was soon far ahead of the little spike bucks. It looked as though another suitor would lose his life and Coyote would become wealthier than ever, but about this time the great, strong medicine began to take effect. The girl's feet and legs grew numb. She began to stumble along. The little spiked bucks caught up with her, passed her, and easily led her to the finish. She became the wife of Mountain Goat and went to live with him at the head of Lake Chelan.

Coyote was lonesome after the girl left. Moreover, he was very lazy and hated to do house-work. His house soon became too filthy to live in. He determined to journey to the head of the lake, kill his son-in-law, and bring his daughter back to the Flats to keep house for him. He traveled overland to the head of the lake and arrived at the Goat's house. He entered and looked about the premises, trying to figure out the best means of dispatching Mountain Goat. He might have succeeded in his wicked plan, but in the Goat's house lived the little Coney or Rock Rabbit. Now the Coney could read a person's thoughts. As Coyote stood there planning how to dispose of Mountain Goat she read his thoughts and repeated them aloud, disclosing his intention to kill his son-in-law and take his daughter back to Brewster with him.

This disclosure of his intentions so discomfited Coyote that he left hurriedly, slinking back to his home on Brewster Flat. Yes, he used to live right here on the Flats a long, long time ago. Those huge boulders are his cooking baskets.

Harold Cundy, "Rock Pictures of North Central Washington," unpublished manuscript, 1938, Washington State Historical Society.

Figure 30. Drawings by Harold J. Cundy, 1936. *Washington State Historical Society*

river mile 530

Plate 102. Innomoseecha in dugout canoe with centennial flagpole of old Fort Okanogan in background; view taken from the right bank of the Okanogan River.
Asahel Curtis (#30111), Washington State Historical Society

Part III Okanogan River to Spokane River

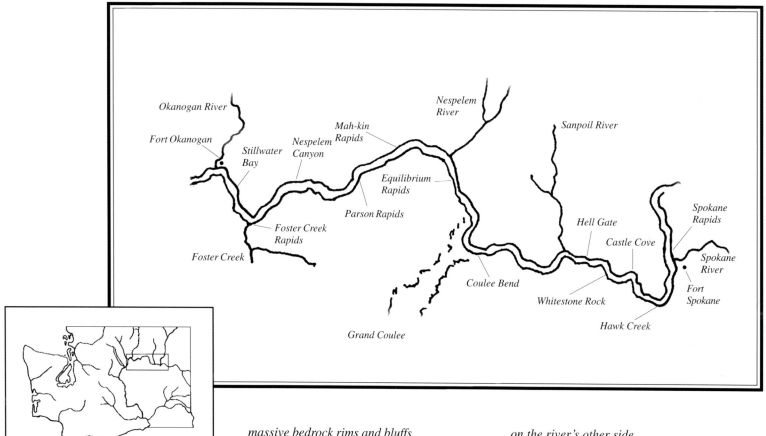

massive bedrock rims and bluffs
presenting views into the canyon below

on one side a long trench where
an ancient micro-continent
separated by a thousand miles
came to join the mainland

on the river's other side
cliffs with shoulders of molten rock

the deep canyon, its boulders, cobbles, and stone
scattered by glacier and flood
fierce fast water and a steady noise
now only the sound of wind remains

wdl

Confluence of Okanogan and Columbia Rivers

A village of the Southern Okanogan Indians, *T'kuya·'tum* (people at the mouth of the river), was situated near the mouth of the Okanogan River. On the last day of August 1811, life in the village changed forever with the arrival of American fur-traders Alexander Ross and David Stuart in two dugout boats. The meeting was made all the more poignant by the appearance of a brilliant comet in the western nighttime sky.

The fur-trading party's boats were packed with 1 1/2 tons of supplies belonging to Astor's Pacific Fur Company bound for the upper Columbia. Stored within one of these packs was an American flag that by September was flying over newly established Fort Okanogan, situated a half mile from where the Okanogan met the Columbia. Built of driftwood, Fort Okanogan was the third Euro-American settlement in Washington. (The Spanish had temporarily occupied Neah Bay in 1792, and the Canadians had established Spokane House in 1810.)

Over the first winter, Ross collected more than 1,500 beaver pelts for shipment downriver. Soon Fort Okanogan became the major meeting point for pack trains heading to and from New Caledonia (present day British Columbia) and for brigades of boats traveling up and down the Columbia. The Astorians' presence here, however, was short-lived; two years later (1813) the Pacific Fur Company sold its holdings to the North West Company of Canada. A new fort was constructed by the "Nor'westers" in the summer of 1816. Five years later, at the direction of the Crown, the North West Company and the Hudson's Bay Company settled long-standing differences and combined into one firm. By

1830, the fur-trading business was peaking. In the 1830s, a third fort was constructed southeast on a bluff overlooking the river. This offered both a better landing site and relief from the mosquito-laden slough below. Trade, however, diminished over the years. The last pack train traveled over the old Okanogan Trail in 1847, thus ending a colorful era in the river's history.

Chelan Indian Long Jim (Innomoseecha) and his family were given title to the land following the closing of the fort. Here he kept cattle and ferried people across the Columbia.

Opposite: **Plate 103.** Confluence of Okanogan and Columbia rivers, ca. 1907. *Photographer unknown, George Wilson Collection*

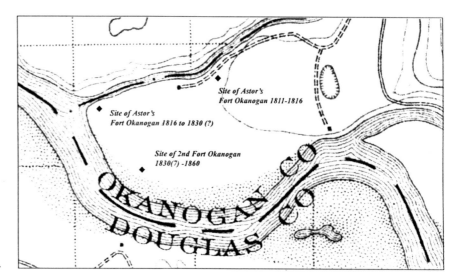

Figure 31. USGS map, Okanogan Quadrangle, 1905.

Stillwater Bay

Plate 104. View of Stillwater Bay, two miles below Bridgeport, taken from left bank looking downriver, 1891.
O.C. Yocum, National Archives
(77H 615 P-38)

Stillwater Bay marked the end of relatively smooth water for upriver traffic before approaching the foot of Foster Creek Rapids and the Nespelem Canyon. In the distance is Buena Bar, where the Columbia turned north, passing the old Port Columbia ferry crossing before meeting the Okanogan River.

Foster Creek Rapids

Plate 105. Foster Creek Rapids (future site of Chief Joseph Dam), from left bank looking upriver, 1891.
O.C. Yocum, National Archives (77H 615 P-40)

Early surveyors classified Foster Creek Rapids as among the most hazardous on the river. The 3-mile run, with a drop of more than 20 feet, cascaded through crooked channels, around boulders, and over jagged rocks. Early settlers recalled frequently seeing native encampments near where Foster Creek enters the Columbia. In 1879, the U.S. Army, under the direction of Lt. Symons, developed a military road from Ritzville to the mouth of Foster Creek. During the following winter, 1879-80, the Second U.S. Infantry camped on the flat below the creek. In 1880, these soldiers established the short-lived post on Lake Chelan. Mary Proff Smith, one of Bridgeport's first residents, fondly remembered catching trout with her bare hands at the waterfall close to where the creek joins the river.

river mile 546

Plate 106. Foster Creek Rapids, from left bank looking upriver, 1908.
B.C. Collier, National Archives, Pacific Alaska Region

Plate 107. Foster Creek Rapids,
from right bank, 1909.
Fred McDermott, Wenatchee World

River improvements on the Mid-Columbia had begun at Priest Rapids in 1891, but were slow to come above the Okanogan. In 1903, U.S. Senators Ankeny and Foster, accompanied by other dignitaries, completed a nine-day inspection from Wenatchee to Kettle Falls aboard the *Alexander Griggs.* Several years later, Congress authorized a new survey. By January 1908, U.S. Army engineers boarded the *Enterprise* and proceeded upriver as far as Grand Rapids in "simply abominable" weather. Their report was favorable, but no money was budgeted for improvements. Finally, through the efforts of state legislators and the untiring advocacy of regional promoters W.D. Lyman and Dr. N.G.

Blalock, the State of Washington authorized $50,000 for river work in 1909 under the direction of Captain Fred McDermott. The federal government added to this funding in 1910, and by April 1911 McDermott had completed the work.

The rock obstruction shown above stood in 20 feet of water at the head of Foster Creek Rapids. Workers strung cables to get on and off the rock and used a miner's cage to drill holes and set dynamite charges. The ensuing explosion sent debris hundreds of feet into the air and was felt 25 miles away.

Mildred McDermott, 1910

*T**he water was high and the current swift one night as the Yakima sped through a narrow channel. Great boils bubbled out and over, spilling themselves back into the river.... Mother and we children, all small, had gone to bed. Days were tiring for all of us. On a river steamer, there were so many dangerous places for children to play: near the open hatch back aft, on the Texas deck which had no railing. There were hog chains to trip over. The freight deck was stacked with crates of heavy machinery and sacks of wheat. Everyone, including the crew, felt relieved when they knew we children were asleep.*

Captain McDermott, my father, was a veteran river man. He knew every curve in the shoreline, every protruding or partially submerged rock, every sandbar and every eddy. Their locations were dependable. But the ferry cables were not. Although "Cap," as he was widely known, knew where ferries crossed the Columbia, he could never be sure just how far above the water surface their cables might be at any given time. Often the ferrymen neglected to tighten

Plate 108. *Yakima* at Foster Creek, 1909. Wenatchee World

Above Foster Creek

their cables when the river rose.... Since "Cap" knew in this stretch of the river that he was approaching a ferry, he peered steadily forward. A rusty black cable is difficult to see at night, even if it is illuminated by a short-ranged searchlight.

Suddenly, Captain McDermott saw a hazy dark streak, sagging directly in line with his vessel's jackstaff. To pass beneath it, a dramatic change in the Yakima's course would be necessary. He gave the wheel a rapid turn to starboard. Then, as he reached to pull a slow bell, he glanced aft to see how the boat was responding to the rudder. On top of the railing above the paddle wheel, he saw a small white object silhouetted against the spray. He blinked his eyes and looked again. It was his 4-year old son Paul, clad in pajamas.

Forgetting the peril of the Yakima "Cap" dashed out of the pilot house, jumped to the Texas deck, raced across it with long strides, leaped to the cabin deck, and ran toward the railing with outstretched arms. Just as he reached the boy, who stood facing the churning paddles, the boat headed into a cross current and the unattended pilot wheel spun back to port. The jerk overbalanced Paul. As he started to plunge, "Cap" caught him around the knees. Together they fell on the deck. Paul awakened by the impact, asked sleepily, "What are you here for, Papa?" The answer was a tight hug.

As "Cap" started to rise, he heard a crash of cracking timber and felt a terrific jar. Looking up, he saw the jack staff—a pole at the bow from which a flag could be flown— being hurled into the river. The ferry cable was moving onward like a keen edged scythe. It grazed the pilot house roof, snapping off the steam whistle which fell with a sharp, metallic ring. It slashed into the smokestack, throwing pieces in all directions. It passed over the stern and was gone. The remnants of the smokestack spat forth a shower of big, unscreened glowing cinders.

The two deckhands came running out of their quarters as Paul's mother emerged from the cabin. She looked in bewilderment at her little boy and his father. "Oh, my dears," she exclaimed. "Cap" carefully laid Paul in her arms. Then, he quickly ascended the ladder, walked under the burning cinders, and stepped over pieces of the smokestack on the Texas deck. He climbed the next ladder and went into the pilot house to regain control of the Yakima. An excited voice coming through the tube from the engine room greeted him: "Cap, Cap, what's she doing, sinking?" "Cap" calmly rang a stop gong and replied, "Thank God, he's all right. Stand by the engines. We're tying up here."

The engineer wondered why the captain used the wrong gender for a boat. He didn't realize "Cap" was referring to his son.

Mildred McDermott, "Capt. Fred McDermott, Last of the Riverboat Captains," *Okanogan County Heritage*, Fall 1987.

Plate 109. Eagle Rapids, from right bank looking upriver, 1891.
O.C. Yocum, National Archives (77H 615 P-37)

Plate 110. Nespelem Canyon, from left bank looking upriver, 1891 (river mile 554).
O.C. Yocum, National Archives (77H 615 P-35)

Four miles long with a drop of nearly 30 feet, the rough water in Nespelem Canyon included Eagle Rapids, Box Canyon, Whirlpool Rapids, Kalichen Rock, Long Rapids, and White Cap Rapids. Surveyor William Cuthbert measured the low-water current at 10 miles-per-hour, but thought the river would run much faster when the water was higher. Jutting rocks twisted the channel into a "Z" shape, tossing frothing water from one wall of the canyon to the other. Kalichen Rock, composed of honeycombed basalt, obstructed the middle of the channel at the foot of Long Rapids. Behind it was an extremely dangerous whirlpool nearly extending across the river. During high water, its magnitude and power increased, causing it to swallow most objects coming downriver. Witnesses reported seeing 250-foot trees spiraling down into its vortex and not resurfacing until a half-mile further downriver. At most places along the Columbia, the normal seasonal rise of water was 10 to 12 feet, but in Box Canyon it measured 50 to 90 feet above low-water levels. During high water the river was backed up nearly 10 miles toward Coulee Bend.

A small village of Southern Okanogans, *kali'tcmen* (big rapids), once bordered the lower canyon.

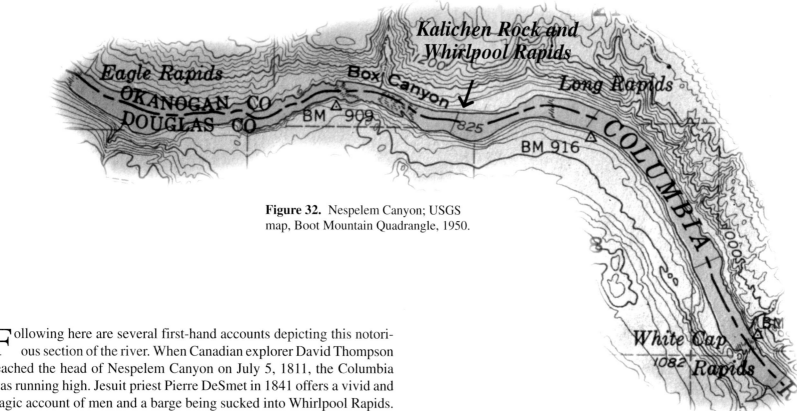

Figure 32. Nespelem Canyon; USGS map, Boot Mountain Quadrangle, 1950.

Following here are several first-hand accounts depicting this notorious section of the river. When Canadian explorer David Thompson reached the head of Nespelem Canyon on July 5, 1811, the Columbia was running high. Jesuit priest Pierre DeSmet in 1841 offers a vivid and tragic account of men and a barge being sucked into Whirlpool Rapids. DeSmet names an Iroquois Indian, Pierre, who saved himself by hanging onto floating bedding. He likely is the same "Old Pierre" who guided Lt. Symons's boat past Kalichen Rock in 1881.

Amazingly, steamboats managed to ascend the rapids for a short period after 1907. Most were piloted by Captain Fred McDermott, a man having an enormous passion for navigating the upper Columbia. Steamboating here was made far easier following a successful attempt to persuade both the State of Washington and the U.S. government to fund removal of the most dangerous obstacles in the canyon. Apparently, whitewater boatman M.J. Lorraine, when traveling downriver in 1921, did not know about McDermott's channel improvement work. Lorraine reported that he did not encounter hazards that the Symons report described; neither could he understand why Symons had thought the passage so difficult.

Box Canyon

David Thompson, 1811

*A*s evening approaches it begins to rain. Thompson and his men have entered Box Canyon, where the river drops more than 30 feet in a two-mile run. Darkening walls rise precipitously from the river, and several crew-members walk ahead in search of a campsite. They find only steep banks and wet boulders, no level ground on which to pitch their cotton tents. Meanwhile, Ignace, the steersman, and several others attempt to paddle the boat down the shoreline in order to meet those who have walked ahead. Suddenly, the current thrusts the boat into an overhanging tree that knocks Ignace overboard into the raging waters. The men in the boat respond immediately by paddling into the fast water after him and miraculously, he is rescued. Once safely ashore it is discovered that Ignace has received a severe blow to the head. Thompson bleeds the wound.

Opposite: **Plate 111.** Box Canyon, from right bank looking downriver, 1891. Thompson's small party portaged their equipment along the terrace to the left. *O.C. Yocum, National Archives* (77H 615 P-36)

Night comes and the rain continues without a lull as the men sit shelterless on the rocks through the long hours of darkness.

It is still raining in the morning. Finding driftwood along the shore, the men make two paddles to replace those broken the day before. Thompson reflects on the Sanpoil prayers and dances held for him the previous day. The prayers, "that they might be preserved on the Strong Rapids," will be needed today. Soon the boat is packed tightly and launched into the current, which proves too strong. An order is given to pull ashore, and the men begin unloading the gear for a long portage. Climbing out of the canyon, one of the crew glances up through the mist to see a large procession of men, women, and children, approaching on foot and horseback. They are a welcome sight.

After a brief exchange of formalities the native people enthusiastically help Thompson load his supplies on their horses. Soon the remarkable entourage arrives at their village near the foot of the canyon. Through his Sanpoil interpreters Thompson learns that the people here call themselves Inspaelis. They present Thompson with five horses, five roasted salmon, dried meat, and three bushels of dried roots. Thompson is generous in return. Having good trade relations with these people is essential. In exchange for the horses and other goods, Thompson gives them three feet of tobacco, six feet of beads, nine feet of cloth trim, fourteen rings, four papers of vermilion paint, four awls, six buttons, and eighteen hawkbells.

Adapted from William D. Layman, "Hawkbells: David Thompson in North Central Washington," *Columbia Magazine*, Winter 1991.

Jesuit Priest Pierre DeSmet, 1841

Never shall I forget the sad and fatal accident which occurred on the second day of our voyage at a spot called the "Little Dalles" [Nespelem Canyon]. I had gone ashore and was walking along the bank, scarcely thinking what might happen; for my breviary, papers, bed, in a word, my little all, had been left in the barge. I had proceeded about a quarter of a mile, when seeing the bargemen push off from the bank and glide down the stream with an easy, careless air, I began to repent having preferred a path along the river's side, so strewn with fragments of rocks that I was compelled at every instant to turn aside or clamber over them. I still held on my course, when all at once, the barge is so abruptly stopped that the rowers can hardly keep their seats. Regaining, however, their equilibrium, they ply the oars with redoubled vigor, but without any effect upon the barge. They are already within the power of the angry vortex:

the waters are crested with foam; a deep sound is heard which I distinguish as the voice of the pilot encouraging his men to hold to their oars to row bravely.

The danger increases at every minute, and in a moment more all hope of safety has vanished. The barge, the sport of the vortex, spins like a top upon the swirling waters—the oars are useless—the bow rises—the stern descends, and the next instant all have disappeared. A deathlike chill shot through my frame—a dimness came over my sight as the cry, "We are lost!" rung in my ears, and told but too plainly that my companions were buried beneath the waves.

Overwhelmed with grief and utterly unable to afford them the slightest assistance, I stood a motionless spectator of the tragic scene. All were gone, and yet upon the river's breast there

was not the faintest trace of their melancholy fate. Soon after the whirlpool threw up, in various directions, the oars, poles, the barge capsized, and every lighter article it had contained. Here and there I beheld the unhappy bargemen vainly struggling in the midst of the vortex. Five of them sunk never to rise again. My interpreter had twice touched bottom and after a short prayer was thrown upon the bank. An Iroquois saved himself by means of my bed; and a third was so fortunate as to seize the handle of an empty trunk, which helped him sustain himself above water, until he reached land.

The rest of our journey was more fortunate. We stopped at forts Okinakane and Wallawalla [sic], where I baptized several children.

Pierre DeSmet, *Travels in the Far West*, edited by Reuben Gold Thwaites (1906).

Opposite: **Plate 112.** Box Canyon above Whirlpool Rapids, from left bank looking upriver, ca. 1921.
John Jay Browne Collection, Wenatchee Valley Museum and Cultural Center

river mile 556

Plate 113. Kalichen Rock within Long Rapids, from left bank looking upriver, 1891.
O.C. Yocum, National Archives *(77H 615 P-33)*

Kalichen Rock

Lt. Thomas W. Symons, 1881

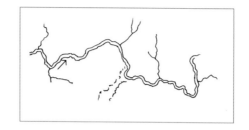

The river is here contracted in width and the banks are steep and rocky. A little below, the shores are strewn with huge masses of black basaltic rock of all sizes and shapes, and this continues for several miles, forming a characteristic picture of Columbia River scenery. The complete silence and lifelessness added to the scene makes it exceedingly wild, almost unearthly. And so we plunge along swiftly through the rolling water, with huge rocks looming up, now on one side and then on the other. Every stroke of the oar is bearing us onward, nearer and nearer, to that portion of our voyage most dreaded, the terrible Kalichen Falls and Whirlpool Rapids. We hear the low rumbling of the water, and see the tops of the huge, half-sunken rocks and the white foam of the troubling waters. For a few moments the rowing ceases, while brave old Pierre gives his orders to the Indians in their own tongue. He knows that everything depends upon his steering and their rowing or backing at the right moment, with all the strength that they possess. Years ago he was in these very rapids, and out of a crew of sixteen men, eight perished in the water and on the rocks.

The Indians make their preparations for the struggle by stripping off all their superfluous clothing, removing their gloves, and each ties a bright-colored handkerchief tightly about his head; poles and extra oars are laid ready in convenient places to reach should they become necessary, and then with a shout the Indians seize their oars, and commence laying to them with all their strength. We are rushing forward at a fearful rate, owning to the combined exertions of the Indians and the racing current, and we shudder at the thought of striking any of the huge black rocks near which we glide. Now we are fairly in the rapids, and our boat is rushing madly through the foam and billows; the Indians are shouting at every stroke in their wild savage glee; it is infectious; we shout too, and feel the wild exultation which comes to men in moments of great excitement and danger.

Ugly masses of rock show their heads above the troubled waters on every side, and sunken rocks are discernible by the action of the surf. Great billows strike us fore and aft, some falling squarely over the bow and drenching us to the waist. This is bad enough, but the worst is yet to come as we draw near with great velocity to a huge rock which appears dead ahead.

Has old Pierre seen it? The water looks terribly cold as we think of his failing eyesight. Then an order, a shout, backing on one side and pulling on the other, and a quick stroke of the steering oar and the rock appears on our right hand. Another command, and answering shout, and the oars bend like willows as the Indians struggle to get the boat out of the strong eddy into which Pierre had thrown her. Finally she shoots ahead and passes the rock like a flash, within less than an oar's length of it, and we shout for joy and breathe freely again. This eddy becomes in a high stage of water a veritable whirlpool, with the well at its center many feet in depth. Hence the name Whirlpool Rapids.

Lieutenant Thomas W. Symons, Chief Engineer of the Department of the Columbia, *Report of an Examination of the Upper Columbia River and the Territory in its Vicinity in September and October, 1881* (Washington, D.C., 1882).

Gaviota Bend

Cuthbert Survey, 1891

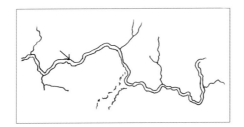

With the growth of new settlements, strengthened by mining strikes in the Okanogan and the success of bringing sternwheelers above Rock Island Rapids, Congress in 1890 authorized $10,000 for a complete survey of the Columbia River from the International Boundary to Rock Island Rapids. William Cuthbert was placed in charge, under the direction of Thomas W. Symons, who by now had been promoted from lieutenant to captain. Cuthbert's orders were to: 1) secure data for a topographical representation of the river; 2) determine the nature and extent of all obstructions to the free navigation of the river; and 3) assess the character and amount of work needed to remove those obstructions.

Traveling from Portland to Spokane, Cuthbert organized a fully outfitted crew of twelve men and arranged for the building of boats. Fieldwork began in early March 1891, and was completed to the Okanogan River by the end of December. Maps were drawn to a scale of 2,000 feet to the inch, with principal rapids depicted at 400 feet to the inch. Two photographers accompanied the survey to visually document the river's character. George Warren of Greysville, Illinois, served during the first part of the survey season, taking seventy-one photos from the International Boundary to the Spokane River. O.C. Yocum of Portland joined the survey in September and photographed forty-four views of the Columbia between the Spokane and Okanogan rivers. Five sets of selected photographs were prepared, with one set exhibited at the 1894 Chicago World's Fair.

The distance from the International Boundary to the Okanogan River was established at 214 miles. The surveyors calculated the river's volume to be from 50,000 cubic feet per second at low water, to over 300,000 feet at high water. The average velocity of the Columbia was determined to be 3.5 miles per hour, with many places measuring much higher. The fall of this section of river was 534.4 feet, with an average drop of 2.5 feet per mile. Kettle Falls alone dropped 33 feet at low-water stages. Below Spokane Rapids, the crew measured sections of whitewater falling 6 and 7 feet per mile.

Cuthbert counted 1,948 Colville Reservation Indians living in the fertile valleys and flats along the right bank of the river. No mention was made of the Chinese or their camps, although pioneer accounts indicate Asians still were working the river at this time.

Cuthbert determined that the river could be made navigable for about $18,000,000. The estimate included removing 48,000 cubic yards of rock and building twelve dams with locks at difficult places along the river.

The survey's journal reveals that days were spent running lines, measuring current velocities, mapping, and securing firewood and supplies. Surveyors used a large raft built at Fort Spokane for the supply and cook tent. The crew had the challenge of bringing the raft and boats through some of the most turbulent sections of the Columbia. The weather deteriorated in December to the point that there was snow on the ground when Yocum prepared his glass plates at Foster Creek.

Opposite: **Plate 114.** Cuthbert survey crew at Gaviota Bend, from right bank looking upriver, 1891.
O.C. Yocum, National Archives (77H 615 P-29)

river mile 560

Parson Rapids

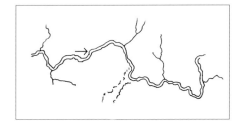

Plate 115. Parson Rapids, from right bank looking upriver, 1891.
O.C. Yocum, National Archives (77H 615 P-28)

William Cuthbert measured the current at Parson Rapids at 6 miles-per-hour and described the channel as being full of rocks. From 3 miles below Parson Rapids to the head of Mah-kin Rapids, a distance of 10 miles, the Columbia had a fall of 41 feet at low water. Cuthbert remarked that the many large basalt boulders on the hillsides reminded him of an enormous herd of bison.

Mah-kin Rapids

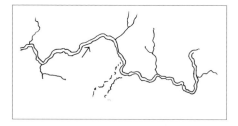

Plate 116. Mah-kin Rapids, from left bank looking upriver, 1891.
O.C. Yocum, National Archives (77H 615 P-27)

For a half mile, the river at Mah-kin Rapids narrowed down sharply between steep banks and increased in speed to more than 10 miles-per-hour. To river adventurer Lewis Freeman, it seemed as if large boulders from the surrounding hills had rolled down into the middle of the channel. In 1881, Lt. Symons reported that the river's shores were strewn with black basalt rocks of all sizes and shapes, forming a "characteristic picture of Columbia River scenery."

river mile 573

Equilibrium Rapids

Plate 117. Equilibrium Rapids, from right bank looking upriver, 1891.
O.C. Yocum, National Archives (77H 615 P-26)

Hudson's Bay Company fur trader John Work called this place "the Big Stone" and camped below here on August 12, 1828, with a brigade of boats en route to Fort Vancouver. The fur trader remarked in his journal that they had lost time due to the need to gum up "Charlie's" boat. After passing these rapids in 1881, Lt. Thomas Symons named the place Equilibrium Rapids because one of the immense rocks in the channel seemed to be nearly spherical, resting in an apparent state of equilibrium.

Coulee Bend

The northern entrance to the vast Grand Coulee chasm is located some 500 feet above the Columbia's left bank at Coulee Bend. Extending southwest across this part of the Columbia Basin, the Grand Coulee was favored by Native peoples and white fur traders as an overland route between the upper Columbia and the mouth of the Snake River. The coulee is a relatively new feature, having formed only in an eye blink of geological time. Between about 15,500 and 12,500 years ago, dozens of great floods were released from Glacial Lake Missoula by the repeated collapse of glacial dams in the Clark Fork canyon locality along today's Idaho-Montana border. The Columbia could not contain these huge volumes of water and, consequently, new channels—such as Grand Coulee—were cut across the Columbia Basin. The Grand Coulee also was widened and deepened when a lobe of the Cordilleran ice sheet dammed the Columbia below Coulee Bend, forming Glacial Lake Columbia. These backed up waters were diverted southward down the large coulee.

The Missoula floods at times also spilled into Glacial Lake Columbia, magnifying the effects of these catastrophic events. The size of the Missoula floods defies imagination. It would be as though the waters of Lake Erie or Lake Huron suddenly broke free and spilled out onto the

Plate 118. Coulee Bend (future site of Grand Coulee Dam), from left bank looking upriver, ca. 1923.
Harold Simmer, Spokane Public Library, Northwest Room

land. Towering waves of churning icebergs and muddy water reaching depths of 500 feet sped across the Columbia Basin in excess of 50 miles per hour, carving out the vast channeled scablands, Grand Coulee, and other water-carved features. When the continental ice lobes retreated back north from the Columbia, the river re-established itself, following its old riverbed skirting north and west around the immense basalt formations of the Columbia Plateau.

Plate 119. Sanpoil-Columbia confluence, from the Columbia's right bank looking upriver. *Spokane Public Library, Northwest Room*

Confluence of Sanpoil and Columbia Rivers

David Thompson visits the village Npqwilx, 1811

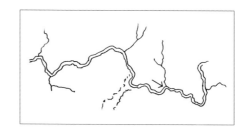

*H*aving pitched our tents by my two Simpoil Natives I sent for the Chiefs of the Village to come and smoke, they came, and the Men followed in single file, and all sat down round the tent; the Chief made a short speech saying he was glad to see us, and then made a present of two half dried Salmon, and about half a bushel of Roots of two kinds.... Four pipes were now lighted and the smoking enjoyed as a feast.... I then explained to them my object to know how this River was to the sea, and if good, very large Canoes with Goods of all kinds would arrive, by which they would be supplied with Clothing and all they wanted if they were industrious hunters.... Smoking for the present being over, permission was asked for the Women to come and see us, which being accorded they soon came with their children, and made us a present of Roots and Berries; and sat down around the Men.... The Chief now proposed they should all dance, to this we assented; the Men formed two slightly curved lines with the women close behind them; they had no instruments and the only music was the song of a man painted Red and Black, his hair stuck full of Feathers. His voice was strong and good, but had few notes; during the song which lasted about eight minutes, the dancers moved very slowly forward with an easy motion, and without changing their position danced back to the place they had left. At the end of the song each person sat down in the place where the song left them: the Chief made a speech of about two minutes; the Song commenced and the dance, and in this manner continued for about an hour when they ended and they retired to their Lodges, and left us to our repose, which we much wanted....

This is the only village of this tribe... they are full sixty men of families and the number of souls about 420.... The Women and children were treated with kind attention, and under all their wants they were cheerful and contented, and I hope we shall soon be able to supply their wants.

David Thompson's Narrative of His Explorations in Western North America, 1784–1812, edited by J.B. Tyrrell (1916).

Hell Gate

The major obstruction to navigation at Hell Gate was caused by a promontory jutting out from the left bank and two large islands, all of granite, located below the promontory. At low and ordinary flows, the current was forced around to the right of the promontory and then almost in a reverse direction back between the promontory and one of the islands. The islands themselves formed a partial dam, creating rapids and rolling breakers between the jutting point and the first island, as well as further downriver. In high water the river flowed through a normally dry channel.

Hell Gate's name reflects its challenge to voyageurs and others passing through this section of river. Anthropologist Verne Ray learned that its Salish name, *Nxoxoyu's,* meant "deep eyes," possibly due to pot holes or kettles that looked like eye sockets, formed by the swirling waters. Coyote was said to have visited here during a long upriver journey. Joe Covington, a Sanpoil elder, shared this story of the origin of Hell Gate:

> *Coyote was traveling up the Columbia, distributing salmon. He got to Hell Gate and decided to build a falls here. Even though he was given a young woman, he got mad, so he never did complete the falls—he kicked them in three places and these are the three channels through which the Columbia used to flow here.*

A favorite fishing spot was situated a short distance downstream from Hell Gate. The river bottom there was white, making it an excellent place to see and spear salmon from the shore.

Figure 33. Alfred Downing, Map #8 of Upper Columbia, 1881. Detail is from the William Cuthbert Survey of 1891; lines show point of view of photograph to the right, and the arrow indicates the location of the dry channel.

Opposite: **Plate 120.** Hell Gate, from the left bank looking across the river, 1908. Note sternwheeler *Enterprise* between an island and the north shore. *B.C. Collier, National Archives, Pacific Alaska Region*

river mile 619

Whitestone Rock

Lt. Thomas W. Symons, 1881

*A*bout eight miles farther on we come to the Whitestone, a noted land-mark consisting of a gigantic grayish-white rock 500 feet high, standing perpendicularly up from the water on the left bank of the river, partially detached from the rocks to the rear. It is split down the middle by some great contusion. The Indians have a legend concerning this rock of which skunk is the hero.

It would seem that in the long ago a skunk, a cayote (sic), and a rattle-snake each had a farm on the top of the Whitestone. These were the days before the skunk was as odorous as he is now, but was esteemed a good fellow and pleasant companion by other animals. As in some other small communities, jealousies, dissentions, and intrigues arose in this one. The result was that the cayote and rattlesnake took a mean advantage of the skunk one night when he was asleep, and threw him off the rock, away down into the river. He was not drowned, however, but floated on and on, far away to the south and west, until he came to the mouth of the river, where lived a great medicine man and magi-cian. To him the skunk applied and was fitted out with an apparatus warranted to give immunity from, and conquest over, all his enemies. Back he journeyed along the river to his old home, where he arrived, much to the surprise of the cayote and rattlesnake, and commenced to make it so pleasant for them with his pungent perfumery apparatus, the gift of the magician, that they soon left him in undisputed posses-sion of his rock home, which he has maintained ever since.

Close by stood another rock, now inundated, that resembled the shape of a skunk with tail uplifted, pointing to Whitestone Rock.

Lieutenant Thomas W. Symons, Chief Engineer of the Department of the Columbia, *Report of an Examination of the Upper Columbia River and the Territory in its Vicinity in September and October, 1881* (Washington, D.C., 1882).

Plate 121. Whitestone Rock, from left bank looking downriver, 1891.
O.C. Yocum, National Archives (77H 615 P-23)

river mile 626

Castle Cove

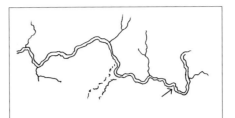

The river now becomes very deeply encañoned with steep, rocky, and in some cases, perpendicular bluffs, on one or both sides. The cañon is in many places very beautiful; the rocks composing the bluffs are many-colored, black, brown, pink, and white, and have many patches of bright red and yellow moss. To this must be added the green of the trees, of which all shades, from the darkest to the brightest, appear; the bright autumnal tints of the bushes, and beyond, above, and about all, the old gold of the withered bunch-grass shining in the sunlight.

The rocks take all imaginable forms, showing up as pinnacles, terraces, perpendicular bluffs, devils-slides, and giants' causeways, the whole forming one of the grandest, most beautiful sights in the universe.

Lt. Thomas W. Symons, 1881

Opposite: **Plate 122.** Castle Cove, from left bank looking upriver, 1891.
O.C. Yocum, National Archives (77H 615 P-22)

129

Plate 123. Peach, from right bank looking across the river.
Jim Black Collection, Wenatchee Valley Museum and Cultural Center

At Hawk Creek, the south-flowing Columbia meets the vast basalt formations of the Columbia Plateau and abruptly turns west. Here, one of the region's first white settlers, John "Virginia Bill" Covington, opened a trading post, selling goods to Indians and Chinese miners. Covington married Spillkeen, a Sanpoil, who when visited by Jesuit Alexander Diomedi in 1879, angrily confronted the priest for preaching against native beliefs.

Confluence of Hawk Creek and Columbia River

Winters generally were mild along this section of the river, making it prime land for fruit orchards. In 1894, Elmer Smith purchased 5,000 acres on the bench just above the river. Eventually eleven families settled in the community of Peach, which was known for commercially growing pears, peaches, apples, and prunes. In his late 80s, Smith recounted how, on a quiet day, one could hear the distant rumble of Hell Gate 16 miles downriver.

Plate 124. Spokane-Columbia confluence.
U.S. Bureau of Reclamation

Plate 125. Spokane Rapids with Cuthbert's survey boat descending the river, 1891; from right bank looking upriver.
O.C. Yocum, National Archives (77H 615 P-20)

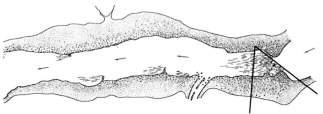

Point of view of photograph to right.

Figure 34. Spokane Rapids.
1891 Cuthbert Survey

132

Confluence of Spokane and Columbia Rivers
Spokane Rapids

M. J. Lorraine, a self-styled old voyageur and whitewater man, constructed a boat at the headwaters of the Columbia River in 1921 and proceeded downriver. He describes Spokane Rapids in his book, *The Columbia Unveiled* (1924):

The River is somewhat contracted here, the rapids about a mile long and straight and the shores are covered with great blocks of basalt, many as large as a small cottage. The agitated current starts at the right-hand shore, runs diagonally to the middle of the River, where the breakers become high and tempestuous. Between the line of great breakers and the right-hand shore the water is agitated, but devoid of obstructing rocks, and the waves but moderate. My inspection convinced me that the way to run Spokane Rapids was to cut quickly through the streak of rough water at its beginning, get into the milder waves below, and hug the right-hand shore.

William Cuthbert measured the current here at a fast 15.38 miles-per-hour. From Spokane Rapids to Hawk Creek, 8.5 miles downstream, the river dropped over 30 feet and averaged a brisk 10 miles-per-hour.

In 1880, Lt. Symons and Lt. Col. H.C. Merriam selected the site for Fort Spokane on a terrace immediately to the southeast of the Spokane-Columbia confluence. For most of the fort's 19-year military history, life there was quiet, with soldiers engaging in drills, rather than conflicts. The fort closed its doors in 1899 and was converted into a boarding school for Indian children. Later, the buildings and grounds served as a hospital and tuberculosis sanatorium for Native Americans.

A Sanpoil winter village named *Snkilt* (above the rapids) was located a short distance up the Columbia. In 1978, Louie Pichette recounted the following legend about the turbulent waters of the Spokane Rapids:

There was a Water-Monster who used to kill people in the rapids at snkilt. He lived under the water and he killed people by pulling them down in a whirlpool. Coyote knew this. He had a plan to beat this monster; he got a long tamarack tree and caused it to float sideways down the Columbia River. When they reached the whirlpool, both the tamarack and Coyote were sucked down into it and then swallowed whole by the Water-Monster. Inside, Coyote could see all the animal people and the things that the monster had swallowed. Coyote took his knife and cut at the Water-Monster's heart, but the knife broke, so he cut again. The monster died; as he did so, he opened and closed his anus, which allowed all the animal-people to escape through it. Because this Water-Monster had been killed, it became safe to travel through the rapids at snkilt, although care had to be taken, and it was necessary to use the channel on the west side of the river.

Plate 126. Mitre Rock, campsite of
Cuthbert survey party, July 18, 1891.
*George R. Warren, National Archives,
Pacific Alaska Region*

Part IV

Spokane River to International Boundary

Kootenay arc, old coastal plain
pushed up and folded
leaving a trench between the mainland
and the subcontinent joining it

over laminated quartzite
ice waters forming,
melting and forming again

until the last glacial lake
filled the riverbed
leaving its signature
along the shores

unstable banks of sand and silt
in time break free and fall
giving up one shape
to reveal another

                              wdl

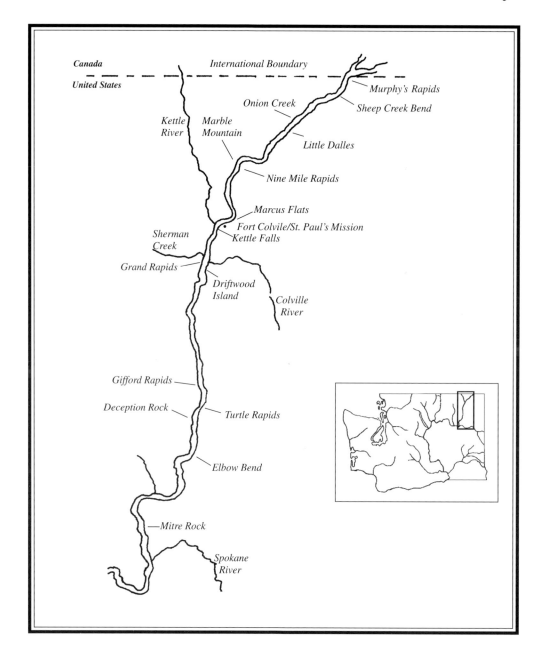

river mile 639–745

Elbow Bend Landslide

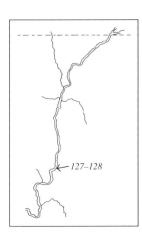

Plate 127. Landslide, from left bank looking downriver.
F. F. Avery Collection, Washington State University Libraries

On the morning of March 26, 1906, an earthquake caused a 60-acre landslide along the west side of the Columbia, stopping the river's flow for several hours and backing it up for miles upstream. According to Colville elder Martin Louie, a man known as Long-Haired Alec was waiting at a deer lick above the unstable formation that morning when the landslide occurred. He proceeded east of the river where he shortly began telling people about what had happened.

Elbow Bend and Hunters Landing

Plate 128. Head of Elbow Bend, from left bank looking across the river, 1891.
George R. Warren, Duke University, Special Collections Library

Plate 129. Hunters Landing, from left bank looking across the river, ca. 1912.
Wenatchee Valley Museum and Cultural Center

The main channel at Elbow Bend followed the right bank and then flowed around several gravel islands in the center of the river. A bar at the foot of the bend caused a strong, but easily negotiated, current. The small towns of Gerome, below Elbow Bend, and Hunters, above it, had their own ferries to transport passengers and supplies to the Colville Indian Reservation. For a short period following 1911, both towns were a popular river stop. In Plate 129, a sternwheeler unloads a school bell and a carriage sits on the foredeck. Boats took on fruit and wheat produced in the rich bottomlands of the Columbia.

river mile 657–660

Deception Rock

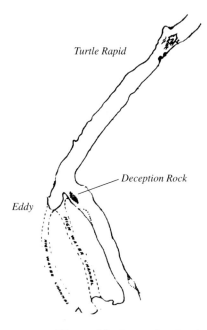

Figure 35. Deception Rock.

Plate 130. Deception Rock, from right bank looking downriver. M.J. Lorraine, *The Columbia Unveiled* (1924).

*O**n an epic journey upriver, Coyote stopped above Deception Rock to barbecue a salmon. Liking the spot, he created a back eddy that collected great numbers of dead fish drifting downstream. Following his meal, Coyote stooped to take a drink of water and a rattlesnake bit his hand, giving the place its Salish name, Skw'i7ikstn (bite hand place).*

Turtle Rapids

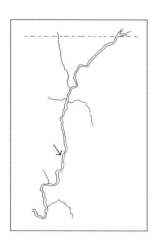

Plate 131. Turtle Rapids, from right bank looking downriver. *B.C. Collier, National Archives, Pacific Alaska Region*

Colville elder Albert Louie recalled a story about Kalispel Indian "Big Louie," who once harpooned and lost a huge salmon at Kettle Falls. Several days later, Indians found the fish at Deception Rock eddy with Big Louie's harpoon still in its back. In Plate 131, Rattlesnake Mountain rises up in the distance behind Turtle Rapids.

river mile 673

Gifford Rapids

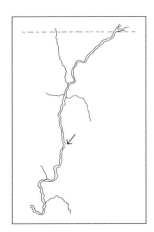

Plate 132. Gifford Rapids, from left bank looking downriver, 1891.
George R. Warren, Duke University, Special Collections Library

The channel through Gifford Rapids was relatively clear at high water, but in low water an exposed ledge extended from the east bank to beyond the center of the river, causing the current to deflect sharply from the ledge into a shallow reef. Making passage even more difficult, the river dropped sharply here, forcing steamboats to execute precise maneuvers to safely bypass the hazard. Captain McDermott cleared Gifford Rapids in 1911 by blasting out the reef.

Driftwood Rocks

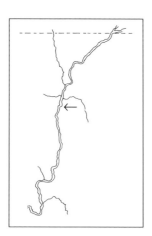

Plate 133. Driftwood Rock, from right bank looking upriver, 1891.
George R. Warren, Duke University, Special Collections Library

This island dividing the river into two channels was named Driftwood Rocks by early surveyors because of the many driftwood logs found there. The site is close to a place where Crawfish responded to Coyote's continual harassment by challenging him to a race. Clamping himself to Coyote's tail, Crawfish taunted Coyote the whole way, causing Coyote to look back the moment they reached the finish line. In so doing, Coyote's tail swung forward and Crawfish seized the opportunity to jump off and win the race.

G rand Rapids, known first as Thompson's Rapids and later as Rickey's Rapids, ran three-fifths of a mile, dropping 20 feet through a rock-studded channel. Canadian engineer J.P. Forde said: "There is no defined channel through them and the river finds its way past them between high, black basaltic rocks strewn around promiscuously in the bed of the river that forms a complete bar to navigation." Surveyor William Cuthbert regarded Grand Rapids as the worst place on the river. An account left by pioneer botanist David Douglas in 1826 indicates the rapids posed little problem to the boatmen of his time.

Plate 134. Grand Rapids, from right bank looking upriver.
J.P. Forde, British Columbia Archives (G-004056)

Grand Rapids

On getting into the current the boats passed along like an arrow from the bow. Half an hour took us to Thompson's Rapids where the water is dashed over scattered rocks, producing an awful agitation of the water from side to side. On being visited by Mr. Pierre L'Etang, the guide, he observed the water was in fine order for jumping the rapids, as he termed it. Good as it appeared to him, I confessed my timidity prevented me from remaining in the boat.... Therefore Mr. Kittson and I walked along the rocks. No language can convey an adequate idea of the dexterity shown by the Canadian boatmen: they pass through the rapids, whirlpools, and narrow channels where, by the strength of such an immense body of water forcing its way, it is risen in the middle to perfect convexity. In such places where you think the next moment you are to be dashed to pieces against the steep rocks, they approach and pass with an indescribable coolness, leaving it behind cheering themselves with an exulting boat-song.

Journal Kept by David Douglas during His Travels in North America, 1823–1827 (London, 1914).

John Rickey, one of the first white settlers in the region, built a small home on the terrace along the river's east bank in 1872, from which he sold provisions to miners and ran supply boats downriver. One of Rickey's customers was Lt. Thomas Symons, who procured an old Hudson's Bay Company bateau in 1881 for use on his downriver survey.

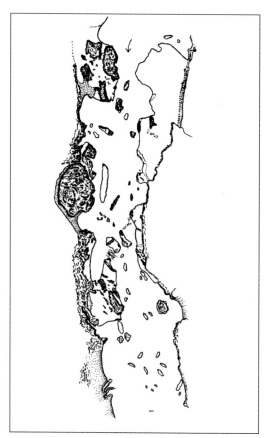

Figure 36. Grand Rapids.
U.S. Army Corps of Engineers, 1914

river mile 697

Captain Fred McDermott, 1911
Centennial Commemoration of David Thompson's Downriver Voyage

The shooting of Rickey Rapids by Captain McDermott in the steamer Shoshone* was an event of such a striking and thrilling nature as to fittingly commemorate the anniversary of the discovery of the falls, celebrated last Friday. The Captain after carefully surveying the rough course he was to take took the Shoshone about half a mile back up stream and maneuvered for a start under full speed in order to enter the channel near the east shore where he had decided was the best and safest course. To avoid certain reefs and eddies at the upper end of the rapids it was necessary to prevent being drawn into the main current, which dashed over a succession of ledges throwing up huge rollers that heaved up and broke in foam through the violence of the current and the immense amount of water. Having attained sufficient speed, which was the best the boat could command, the Captain shot the little steamer over the brink. The resulting sensation was that experienced in descending a swift elevator. The spectators who lined the shore to observe the thrilling spectacle were to have been notified of the start by three shrill blasts on the steamer's whistle, but they could not hear the sound on account of the booming of the waters. The first notice they received was when the boat dashed into view swept along by the current, which added its speed to that of the boat and hurled it along at the rate of five-sixths of a mile a minute. At this speed, which was probably never before attained by any boat on this river, the boat struck the swells, tearing loose part of the front deck. The attitude of the Captain at this time is worthy of preservation in stone or bronze as he stood with an eye fixed on the treacherous current while the spray and dashing water tried in vain to drive him from the tiller. The exciting spectacle was worth traveling thousands of miles to view.

The Scimitar (Kettle Falls newspaper), June 29, 1911.

---

* In a personal communication, the late Captain McDermott's daughter, Mildred McDermott, identified the steamboat as the *Enterprise*.

—WDL

Opposite: **Plate 135.** Grand Rapids, from left bank looking upriver.
Wenatchee Valley Museum and Cultural Center

river mile 697

The Hero of Kettle Falls ~ D.B. Fitzgerald

*T*old by D.B. Fitzgerald, this story describes Ellen Carter, a four-year-old girl who climbed onto a boat along the shoreline above Rickey Rapids. As Ellen crawled to the boat's stern, her weight loosened the hold of the keel upon the gravel. At that moment Mrs. Carter looked up, but the boat already was set adrift. Her frantic cry brought half a dozen people running to the bank, yet all they could do was race along the shore in helpless pursuit. Soon little Ellen's boat was full into the ten mile an hour rapids, tossing and turning as it rushed past rocks through the menacing waves. Now fully into the middle of the river, her boat crashed on the submerged end of a great wedge-shaped rock. Miraculously, Ellen was thrown from the boat onto the boulder's surface. After getting to her feet, she turned toward shore and waved to her mother. Seeing that her daughter was still alive, Mrs. Carter let out a shout of relief yet all remained deeply alarmed as no one had ever survived such a trip through these rapids. She pleaded with the men on the scene, "Oh, do something! Please do something!" Just then Joe Quimby came down to the river having just returned from a hunt. Mrs. Carter ran up to him grabbing his arm with both hands. "Joe!" she cried, in heart-broken appeal,

"Help me, Joe!" Quimby, known as the biggest man at the falls and the strongest of swimmers, drew Mrs. Carter's arms gently aside, fixing his full attention on the rapids. He then turned to several men and ordered, "A couple of you fellows mount your ponies! Ride to Bill Simpkin's down below. Get his boat, row out to the middle of the river and get in line with that rock at the foot of the rapid." The men mounted their horses and dashed away. On shore all waited, knowing full well both the necessity and extreme danger of what Joe planned to do. Mrs. Carter by now had sunk upon the ground sobbing quietly, her face buried in her arms. Quimby fixed a waterproofed hunting bag unto his back and quickly ran upriver a hundred yards. After the men had positioned themselves in Simpkin's boat at the bottom of the rapid, Joe first waded into the river then plunged himself into its cold waters. Soon he too was swept into the boiling currents spinning round and round through the turbulent waters. Onlookers saw his head disappear several times beneath the breakers only to find him resurfacing farther downstream. Now rushing headlong toward the rock upon which Ellen stood, Joe stretched his arms out before him in order to brace himself before hitting the boulder. Like Ellen, Quimby

Figures 37–38. Illustrations from "The Hero of Kettle Falls."

was somehow thrown upon the rock. A cheer went up from the crowd, but it was quickly replaced by silence when the people saw that Quimby wasn't moving. After several long minutes of intense waiting, Joe slowly rose to his feet. One of the men said, "He was just getting his wind," and again the crowd cheered. Meanwhile, Quimby set to work. Taking the rubber bag from his shoulders, he placed Ellen within it and tied the neck of the bag over her head before strapping it tightly to his back. After signaling the men in the boat who were waiting below, Quimby stepped to the lower edge of the rock and jumped into the fast moving waters. In a flash they disappeared amidst the spray and foam, lost to view from the people on shore who looked in vain to find them. The men at the foot of the rapids held their position, paddling with all their might. All at once, one of the men dropped his oars and grabbed hold of Quimby's wrist. After carefully pulling the two aboard, they quickly headed to shore where the crowd anxiously waited. A dozen men rushed into the shallows and lifted Quimby and his precious cargo from the boat. Opening the bag, they took the crying but unharmed girl to Mrs. Carter. Quimby was placed on the grass, his body covered with bruises, his chest showing a wide gash. An elderly doctor on hand checked his vital signs and much to the relief of the crowd, announced that he wasn't dead and that he would recover. Quimby immediately was taken to a nearby house where the physician tended him through the next night. When Joe finally woke, he told the doctor that he felt foolish for being in bed. The doctor, not wanting to disagree with Quimby, nodded, but added, "Prophets may be without honor in their own country all right, but Kettle Falls knows when it's got a hero."

Adapted from D.B. Fitzgerald,"The Hero of Kettle Falls," in *Heroic Adventures* (Perry Mason Press, 1906).

river mile 697

Legend of Kettle Falls ~ Aeneas Seymour (Lakes Tribe)

I am Coyote, the Transformer, and have been sent by Great Mystery, the creator and arranger of the world. Great Mystery has said that all people should have an equal right in everything and that all should share alike. As long as the sun sets in the west this will be a land of peace. This is the commandment I gave to my people, and they have obeyed me.

My people are the Skoyelpi and Snaitcekst Indians, who lived near the Kettle Falls. I gave them that Falls to provide them with fish all their days…. The Falls was surrounded by potholes in which my people cooked their food. When the Hudson's Bay people came they called it the "falls of the Kettle." The traders of the North West Company called it LaChaudiere.

Many generations ago my people were hungry and starving. They did not have a good place to catch their fish. One day while I was out walking I came upon a poor man and his three daughters. They were thin from hunger because they could not get salmon. I promised the old man I would make him a dam across the river to enable him to catch fish, if he would give me his youngest daughter as my wife. The old man agreed to this and I built him a fine falls where he could fish at low water. But when I went to claim the daughter the old man explained that it was customary to give away the eldest daughter first. So I took the oldest daughter and once again promised the man I would build him a medium dam so he could fish at medium water if I could have the youngest daughter. The old man explained again that the middle daughter must be married before the youngest, so I claimed his middle daughter and built him a fine falls where he could fish at medium water.

Shortly after the father came to me and said he was in need of a high dam where he could fish at high water. He promised me his youngest daughter if I would build this. So I built him a third and highest dam where he could fish at high water. And then I claimed the long-waited youngest daughter as my wife.

And now, because I had built the falls in three levels, my people could fish at low, medium, and high water. I had become responsible for my people, and I saw that the fish must jump up the falls in one certain area where the water flowed over a deep depression. I appointed the old man as Salmon Chief, and he and his descendants were to rule over the falls and see that all people shared in the fish caught there.

Adapted from Ruth Lakin, *Kettle River Country* (1987); story told by Aeneas Seymour to Goldie Putnam.

Plate 136. Kettle Falls, from left bank looking upriver.
Photo postcard, Scamahorn Studio, Author's Collection

Plate 137. Kettle Falls, foot of the east channel in the near foreground.
Photo postcard, Author's Collection

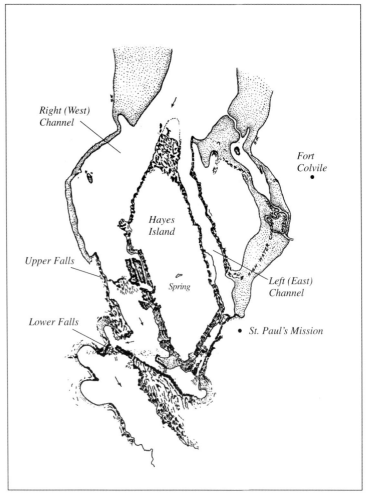

Figure 39. Kettle Falls.
U.S. Army Corps of Engineers, 1914

Plate 138. East channel, upper Hayes Island to left, 1891.
George R. Warren, Duke University, Special Collections Library

At Kettle Falls the Columbia rushed over large, slanted quartzite formations straddling the width of the river. During normal flows, the river divided into two channels separated by Hayes Island. The shallower east channel narrowed to 50 feet before abruptly turning to join the main river channel. The main river dropped 31 feet over two principal falls 1,300 feet apart. The upper falls, extending 380 feet from the west shore to Hayes Island, dropped 18 feet, and the lower falls, formed by a large promontory jutting 60 feet into the river, dropped 13 feet in two parts. After leaping through the lower falls, most salmon swam up the east channel rather than attempting to challenge the upper falls. While the total drop between the two falls remained constant, the lower falls was greater at high water because of the river's engorgement due to the jutting reef. During the great, record-setting 1894 spring runoff, the raging river covered over both falls altogether.

river mile 704

Plate 139. Lower Kettle Falls, from right bank looking across the river at low water, 1923.
Avista Corporation

152

Lower Falls

Plate 140. Lower Kettle Falls, from left bank looking across the river.
Kettle Falls Public Library

*I*n 1880 young Kelly Hill Indian Aeneas Seymour and a cousin were fishing several miles downriver when they saw a man stagger along the shore. To their amazement they learned that two days earlier the man had fallen into the river while fishing at the Lower Falls. Instead of the undertow plunging him to a certain death at the bottom of the river, the current thrust the fisherman backward onto the ledge beneath the falls. Desperate and cold, he pondered his predicament for two days before deciding to leap. Miraculously, currents carried him downstream. When the boys returned to Kettle Falls, the fisherman met relatives and tribal elders who had already begun his funeral preparations.

Story told by Goldie Putnam in Ruth Lakin, *Kettle River Country* (1987).

river mile 704

Plate 141. Upper Kettle Falls, from right bank looking upriver.
Frank Palmer, Kettle Falls Public Library

Opposite: **Plate 142.** Upper Kettle Falls, from right bank looking across the river, ca. 1925.
Avista Corporation

Upper Falls Fieldwork ~ William Cuthbert

*W*ednesday, April 15. Made a sounding lead 12 lbs. in weight. This was necessary, as the currents will sweep away a light one. So being well fixed I took rows of soundings across the pool above the upper falls. This was a dangerous and tedious operation as the boat while in the vicinity of the Falls has to be held by lines from shore. I wanted to know the depth at the base of the rocks causing the fall and at one time I had the boat in the actual suck of the middle of the Fall. Found 60 feet of water above the center of Falls.

William Cuthbert fieldnotes, Record Group No. 77, Seattle District Office, Box 345, National Archives.

Plate 143. Kettle Falls fishing basket.
Kettle Falls Public Library

eginning in late June and continuing through the fall, vast numbers of migratory salmon reached Kettle Falls. Frontier artist Paul Kane in the 1840s compared them to large flocks of birds leaping the falls from dawn to dusk, with as many as forty jumping simultaneously. Fishing here always was dangerous and required a degree of organization that had taken centuries to develop.

A highly respected Salmon Chief, called See-pay or Chief of the Waters, speared the first fish coming upriver and presided over ceremonies honoring the salmon's return. When the water level fell, the Salmon Chief supervised the placement of large, wicker-basket traps alongside the rocks where the fish leapt from the water. It was not unusual to find 300 fish in a basket when it was lifted from the turbulent waters.

Fishermen speared and netted up to 3,000 salmon per day. To prevent the large fish from yanking fishermen into the roiling waters, lines were affixed to harpoons so that if a salmon was not immediately landed, the fish could take the line downstream. When a salmon was speared, the pole was deftly turned to fix the harpoon in the fish's flesh. Often, to prevent being thrown off balance, a fisherman threw himself prone on the suspended platform as he worked to land a fish.

By day's end the Salmon Chief portioned the catch among the families according to their recognized rights and needs. As salmon comprised up to a half of the native diet, families needed to procure from three to six fish per day to sustain them throughout the year.

Figure 40. Chief of the Waters (See-pay).
Stark Museum of Art, Orange, Texas

156

Plate 144. Kettle Falls fishery.
Ellis Morigeau, Teakle Collection, Spokane Public Library Northwest Room

Archaeologist/historian David Chance estimated that prior to 1875, fishermen caught a million pounds of salmon annually at the falls. During salmon runs, Kettle Falls was a place of excitement and festivity, drawing more than a thousand people annually. Camps bustled with activity as a wide array of families shared the work of fishing by day and the pleasures of singing, dancing, and gaming at night.

Ceremony of Tears

On Sunday, June 13, 1941, Indian people from both sides of the border gathered at Hayes Island to honor and grieve—the falls soon would be inundated by Grand Coulee Dam. For three days, many spoke to the memory and meaning of the falls. Among them were Chief Joseph Seymour of Kelly Hill, Sanpoil leaders Jim James and John Frank, and Kalispel chiefs Pete Helakeetsa and Pete Joseph. They spoke of Kettle Falls as a place their people had known since time began—the vital center of a lifeway that had been thousands of years in the making.

Reflecting on the falls fifty years later, historian/archaeologist David Chance wrote:

> *Kettle Falls was the focal point of society and culture, the place of abundance, of great dances and of marathon gambling games in which the wealth and commodities found their way into new channels. It was the largest cluster of villages for more than a hundred miles in every direction, the place to go for variety, for news, for the giving and receiving of gifts both promised and unexpected, the place to hope for a windfall, to discover the prospects for marriage, to look for a relative or friend long lost, or to consult and consort with powerful shamans.*
>
> From *People of the Falls* (Kettle Falls Historical Center, 1986).

Multiple losses were felt that week. It was a particularly sad time for those who had been forced to move their homes from the Grand Coulee Dam reservoir area. The people reflected and prayed—gone the salmon, gone the favorite places along the river where other fish might be caught, gone thousands of acres of bottomlands and access to root and berry grounds.

On July 5, 1941, Kettle Falls disappeared. Its inspiring beauty—the foaming, surging, roaring, tumbling, mists, sprays, and shimmering rainbows in the sunlight—covered beneath the newly created reservoir.

Opposite: **Plate 145.** Gathering at Kettle Falls, 1941.
Wallace Gamble, Northwest Museum of Arts and Culture (L85-143.380)

Hayes Island

river mile 704

St. Paul's Mission

Plate 146. St. Paul's Mission, ca. 1860–61.
Royal Engineers Corps Library, Crown Copyright/MOD

Protestant missionary Samuel Parker visited Fort Colvile in 1836, observing that the natives were friendly and peaceful. Catholic priests followed, with Reverends Francis Blanchet and Modeste Demers baptizing nineteen persons during a brief stay in 1838. Seven years later, Pierre DeSmet supervised the building of Kettle Fall's first mission, "a little chapel of boughs" placed among huts on a prominence overlooking the falls. Another Jesuit, Joseph Joset, erected a sturdier church in 1847, which was christened St. Paul's Mission. Built in the French Canadian "post-on-sill" style, the two-story building consisted of horizontal squared timbers with tongued ends that slid into the grooves of upright

posts. The entire structure was held together by wooden pins rather than iron nails. The mission was active during a time of escalating pressures on native populations, including several deadly smallpox epidemics, an influx of miners following 1855, and increased settlement after 1871 when a U.S. Army post, Fort Colville, was established fifteen miles southeast of the Hudson Bay Company's old Fort Colvile. Soon thereafter, a church built near the new military post led to the decline and abandonment of the older mission. Priests officiated the last services held at St. Paul's during the 1875 fishing season. After years of deterioration, the church was restored at its original location in 1939.

Fort Colvile

Plate 147. Fort Colvile, ca. 1863.
Alexander Gardner, Washington State University Libraries (#97-005)

Fort Colvile, established in 1825 by the Hudson's Bay Company, stood in an expansive prairie immediately east of Kettle Falls. The fort was largely self-sufficient, with up to 340 acres of cultivated land, and about twenty buildings, including cattle barns, horse stables, and pens for chickens, pigeons, and pigs, an officers' quarters, dwelling houses, store, kitchen, Indian hall, blacksmith and carpenter shops, and storage structures for provisions, furs, and ice. Visitors described the fort as a place of refinement and hospitality in the wilderness. Fort Colvile's strategic location made it a principal post for collecting and sending valu-able furs—beaver, badger, bear, fox, lynx, martin, mink, muskrat, otter, raccoon, and wolf—downriver to Fort Vancouver and shipment overseas. Trade remained fairly strong until the Indian wars of 1855–58, after which time the Hudson's Bay Company gradually withdrew its presence in Washington Territory. Provisions in the Treaty of 1846 between the United States and Great Britain had allowed the Hudson's Bay Company to continue occupying the post in American territory. The company finally abandoned Fort Colvile in 1871.

river mile 705

North of Hayes Island

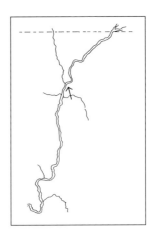

Plate 148. Head of Kettle Falls, from Hayes Island looking upriver, 1891.
George R. Warren, Duke University, Special Collections Library

The earliest artifact assemblages from Hayes Island date from about 8,800 to 9,600 years ago. The archaeological record also shows that the period from 300 to 1400 A.D. was particularly stable and prosperous. Winter pit-houses reveal that the island was used year-round, with people subsisting on salmon, hazelnuts, pine nuts, chokecherries, and camas root. In historic times, members of the Lakes band camped on the island to procure their year's supply of fish.

Confluence of Kettle and Columbia Rivers

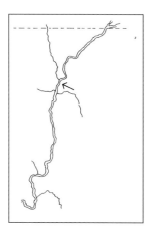

Plate 149. Mouth of the Kettle River in the distance, viewed from the right bank of the Columbia, 1891.
George R. Warren, Duke University, Special Collections Library

The Kettle River watershed encompasses an area of 4,160 square miles, 74 percent of which lies in British Columbia. The river joins the Columbia two miles above Kettle Falls. The stream follows a broad, glaciated trench that provided native populations with natural access to the mountains to the north and from there westward to the Okanogan Valley and its lakes. Stories set in the Ancient Time tell of a Monster living in the canyon near the mouth of the Kettle River. Whenever people attempted to pass, the Monster crushed victims by making the walls of the canyon close in upon them. Using the power of thunder, Coyote permanently pushed the walls out to stop the people-killing Monster.

Marcus Flat

British Boundary Commission, Charles Wilson's Journal

Beginning in the late 1850s, the growing presence of gold miners in British Columbia made it necessary for Great Britain and the United States to define the international boundary line established by the Treaty of 1846. By 1860, survey commissions from both countries were actively working in the rugged terrain of the Pacific Northwest. Charles Wilson, secretary to the British Boundary Commission, writes of his experiences while wintering at Marcus near Fort Colvile:

Now that we are in our winter quarters things go on quietly enough, work all day & a quiet rubber or game of backgammon in the evening, with an occasional visit to the Hudson Bay fort or a drive in a sleigh to break the monotony. We have had some pretty cold weather & a quantity of snow, which lies on the ground, but we are very comfortable & have not felt the cold nearly as bad as we did last year in the Fraser River country. We have not much communication with the outer world. At present our express messenger or postman is nearly a fortnight behind his time & we are beginning to be afraid lest he should have been cut off by Indians or murdered by white men. You can picture the Commission on a winter's evening sitting in a circle round a huge fire of logs, a kettle singing merrily by its side with sundry suspicious looking tumblers standing on a table close by & then the yarns that are told, where everyone has his little troubles & adventures to talk over, of weary nights with mosquitoes, or rattlesnake bed fellows, of onslaughts on grouse, toiling over mountains & fording rapid streams, what one's feelings were when he

Plate 150. Winter quarters at Marcus Flat (old Marcus townsite), British Boundary Commission, 1860–61. *Royal Engineers Corps Library, Crown Copyright/MOD*

saw the mule with all his household property go rolling over a precipice, or another's when he broke the stock of his pet double barrel, all talked & laughed over & often looked back to with a sort of pleasure. On Saturday nights home is the general topic of conversation & we never omit to drink to the health of all our absent friends on that occasion.

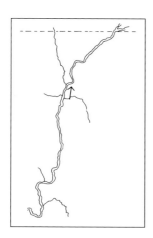

Plate 151. Bend 2.5 miles above Marcus, from left bank looking upriver, 1891.
George R. Warren, Duke University, Special Collections Library

Surveyor William Cuthbert noted that quiet water flowed both above and below these short rapids located upstream from Marcus. George Warren's survey photograph taken in April 1891 shows the river at high water, concealing twenty-three rocks that jutted out from the right shore just below the bend in the river.

river mile 710

Plate 152. Pingstone's Rapids, from left bank looking downriver, 1891.
George R. Warren, Duke University, Special Collections Library

Pingstone's Rapids

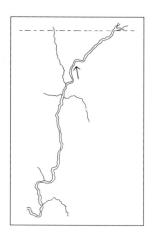

Plate 153. Head of Pingstone's Rapids, from left bank looking upriver, 1891; site of Bossburg. *George R. Warren, Duke University, Special Collections Library*

Pingstone's Rapids was named after Captain Alfred Pingstone, a Lower Columbia River steamboat captain who surveyed the upper Columbia in 1880. The rapids were 2 miles long with a current of 8 miles-an-hour. Large gravel bars divided the river into two channels and there were sixteen small but hazardous boulders standing at the head of the left channel. Cuthbert recommended in 1891 that the boulders be removed for safe steamboat passage, but as D.C. Corbin's railway was scheduled to follow the Columbia north of Pingstone's Rapids, Congress never approved improvement work on this section of river.

river mile 715

Narrow Channel at Marble Mountain

Plate 154. Narrow channel at Marble Mountain, from left bank looking downriver. *George R. Warren, Duke University, Special Collections Library*

Marble Mountain

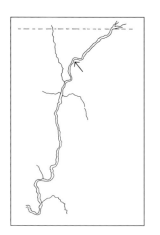

Plate 155. Marble Mountain, from left bank looking across the river.
George R. Warren, Duke University, Special Collections Library

river mile 721

At the head of the Little Dalles, the river narrowed from 800 feet to 196 feet with high, rocky bluffs on both sides. At low water the fall through the rapids was minimal, but at high water the river dropped 20 feet, due to constriction at the head of the rapids. Negotiating the three-quarter mile rapids in high water was extremely hazardous. Boatmen faced the lethal combination of a very crooked channel along with numerous whirlpools capable of swallowing large trees and carrying them one-quarter mile downriver before they resurfaced. Canadian artist Paul Kane visited the Little Dalles in 1847 and recorded the following description of the passage through the rapids:

In going up the river the boats are all emptied, and the freight has to be carried about half a mile over the tops of the high and rugged rocks. One man remains in each boat with a long pole to keep it off from the rocks, whilst the others drag it by a long tow-rope up the torrent. Last year a man, who was on the outside of the rope, was jerked over the rocks by some sudden strain, and was immediately lost. In coming down, however, all remain in the boats; and the guides in this perilous pass, display the greatest courage and presence of mind at moments when the slightest error in managing the frail bark would hurl its occupants to certain destruction. On arriving at the head of the rapids, the guide gets out on to the rocks and surveys the whirlpools. If they are filling in "or making," as they term it, the men rest on their paddles until they commence throwing off, when the guides instantly re-embark, and shove off their boat and shoot through this dread portal with the speed of lightning. Sometimes the boats are whirled round in the vortex with such awful rapidity that it renders the management impossible, and the boat and its hapless crew are swallowed up in the abyss.

Paul Kane, *Wandering of an Artist* (Edmonton, 1974).

The following pages present two accounts depicting the dangers at the Little Dalles. The first recounts the harrowing experience of Captain F.B. Armstrong and a boatman running the rapids by canoe in 1914. The author was George B. Forde, teenage son of Canadian surveyor J.P. Forde, who led a 1914 feasibility study for opening the Columbia from the Canadian boundary south. The second account is journalist Caroline Leighton's description of a failed attempt to bring a steamboat through the Little Dalles in July 1866.

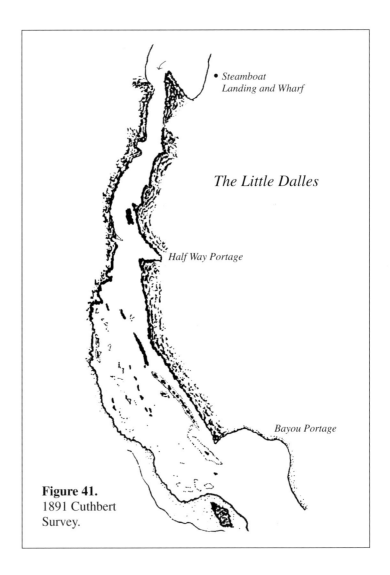

• *Steamboat
Landing and Wharf*

The Little Dalles

Half Way Portage

Bayou Portage

Figure 41.
1891 Cuthbert
Survey.

Opposite: **Plate 156.** Little Dalles, from left bank looking upriver, 1891. *George R. Warren, Duke University, Special Collections Library*

Little Dalles

river mile 729

George B. Forde, 1914

*D*ad *and I walked around while Captain Armstrong and the boatman shot through in the canoe. As Dad and I were up on the cliffs, high above the water we could clearly see our comrades away below us, as they shot into the gorge. As they got fairly into it, traveling at the speed of a racehorse, we on the cliff could see a great whirlpool, which must have measured twelve feet across, about fifty feet ahead of the canoe. As the current was carrying them right towards it they were into it before they had a chance to try to steer out of it. As they got into it they spun completely round in a fraction of a second and then the stern of the canoe began going down, down, down, until it was almost perpendicular, and I thought it was going to disappear altogether. However, the water suddenly threw the canoe right out of the whirlpool again, and it sailed on down with the current. It takes a long time to tell this, but the whole thing happened in about five seconds.*

George B. Forde, "Down the Columbia River by Canoe," British Columbia Archives (MS-0500).

Plate 157. Little Dalles, from right bank looking across the river, 1914. *J.P. Forde, British Columbia Archives (D-00177)*

Opposite: **Plate 158.** Little Dalles, from left bank looking across the river; note the canoe to the right of the large rock, 1914. *J.P. Forde, British Columbia Archives (D-00176)*

river mile 729

Caroline Leighton, 1866

I never saw any river with such a tendency to whirl and fling itself about as the Upper Columbia has. It is all eddies, in places where there is the least shadow of a reason for it.... The most remarkable part of the river is where it is compressed to one-sixth of its width.... When we reached the canon [sic], our real difficulties began. We waited twelve days in the woods for it [the river] to subside.... Everybody grew impatient; and at length one night, the captain said he would try it the next morning, although he had never before been up when the water was so high.... The wildest weather prevailed at this time.... As soon as we went on board, in first starting, a violent thunderstorm came on, lightning, hail, and rain; and a great pine-tree came crashing down, and fell across the bow of the boat.... On this last morning, there were most evident signs of disapproval all about us,—the sky perfect gloom, and the river continually replenishing its resources from the pouring rain, and strengthening itself against us. But we steamed up to the entrance of the canon. Then the boat was fastened by three lines to the shore, and the men took out a cable six hundred feet in length, which they carried along the steep, slippery rocks, and fastened to a great tree. They then returned to the boat, let on all the steam, and began to wind up the cable on the capstan. With the utmost power of men and steam, it was sometimes impossible to see any progress. Finally, however, that line was wound up; and the boat was again secured to the bank, and the cable put out the second time.... We had then wound up two-thirds of the cable. Immediately after, this remarkable occurrence took place: The great heavy line came wholly up out of the water. A bolt flew out of the capstan, which was a signal for the men who were at work on it to spring out of the way. The captain shouted, "Cut the rope!" but that instant the iron capstan was torn out of the deck, and jumped overboard, with the cable attached to it. I felt thankful for it, for I knew it was the only thing that could put an end to our presumptuous attempt.... All day, the rain had

Plate 159. Little Dalles, from right bank looking upriver, 1891.
George R. Warren, Duke University, Special Collections Library

never ceased; and the river had seemed to me like some of those Greek streams that Homer tells of, which had so much personal feeling against individuals. When the capstan disappeared, it was just as if some great river-god, with a whiff of his breath, or a snap of his fingers, had tossed it contemptuously aside. So we turned back defeated.

Caroline Leighton, *Life at Puget Sound: With Sketches of Travel in Washington Territory, British Columbia, Oregon, and California 1865–1881* (Boston, 1884).

174

Plate 160. Little Dalles, from right bank looking across the river, 1891. *George R. Warren, Duke University, Special Collections Library*

Plate 161. Little Dalles, from right bank looking downriver, 1891. *George R. Warren, Duke University, Special Collections Library*

river mile 729

Bay above Little Dalles

Plate 162. The bay above the Little Dalles, from right bank looking across the river, 1891. *George R. Warren, Duke University, Special Collections Library*

steamboat landing and warehouse   store and saloon   cook and eating house   barn and yard

A steamboat landing was established at the Little Dalles to provide a vital link in a transportation route between Spokane, Washington, and Revelstoke, British Columbia. In 1890, D.C. Corbin had finished a rail line from Spokane to the Little Dalles. From the Little Dalles, steamboats carried passengers and freight for the remainder of the distance to Revelstoke. Two years later, the Little Dalles landing was abandoned after Corbin extended the railway eleven miles upriver to Northport.

During its short life, however, the enthusiasm of its frontier inhabitants ran high. Bill Hughes, editor of the *Northport News,* left the following report about the July 4, 1892, dance:

> *Saturday night that was a great affair. Cy Townsend moved his counters back and made room for the dancers. At midnight an elegant supper was served by Purty O'Hare who owned the boarding house. The table*

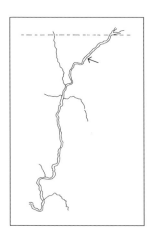

Plate 163. Onion Creek, from left bank looking across at Indian ferry and houses, 1891.
George R. Warren, Duke University, Special Collections Library

groaned under a load of temptingly cooked viands of all kinds.... M.F. Hull of Northport displayed his musical ability on the violin, while others played French harp and bass violin. They appeared a little bashful at the start because they had not played recently, but before quitting time they had it down great. They could dash off "Arkansas Traveler," "Hoe Down Mol," "Dance With the Gal with the Hole in her Stocking," and "Gliding Down De Lane Wid Molly," and other popular numbers in real style.

Onion Creek joined the Columbia a short distance upriver. The 1891 survey map identified the buildings across the river as belonging to Indians.

Sheep Creek Bend

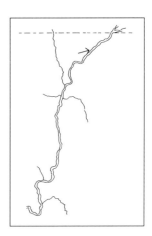

Plate 164. Sheep Creek Bend, from right bank looking across the river, 1891. *George R. Warren, Duke University, Special Collections Library*

Located above the reach of Lake Roosevelt reservoir, Sheep Creek Bend today is relatively unchanged from the time when French Canadian voyageurs plied the Columbia's waters. Situated 9 miles below the international boundary, Sheep Creek joins the Columbia here from the west and Deep Creek from the east, close to two large, rocky islands.

Murphy's Rapids

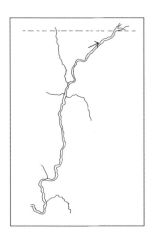

Plate 165. Murphy's Rapids, from right bank looking upriver, 1891. *George R. Warren, Duke University, Special Collections Library*

Surveyor William Cuthbert noted that the Columbia at Murphy's Rapids averaged only 8 feet in depth, but its steady grade allowed for easy passage. One of Cuthbert's crew nearly lost his life here when deciding to swim rather than walk along the rocky shoreline. The swift current carried him a full 2 miles downstream before he finally struggled ashore.

Plate 166. International Boundary, from right bank looking downriver, 1891.
George R. Warren, Duke University, Special Collections Library

Opposite: **Plate 167.** International Boundary, from right bank looking upriver, 1891.
George R. Warren, Duke University, Special Collections Library

In 1846, diplomats in far-off London and Washington, D.C., selected the 49th parallel as the international border in the Columbia watershed. This was a westward extension of the already existing boundary line at the same latitude on the Great Plains. The boundary unavoidably divided the homelands of several indigenous western tribes. Eventually, the 1846 line became the boundary between mainland British Columbia and the states of Washington, Idaho, and Montana—which, along with today's Oregon, once were integral parts of the Old Oregon Country (i.e., the area between 42° and 54°40' north latitude).

At one time, Spain, Russia, Great Britain, and the United States all claimed the Oregon Country. Spanish claims were eliminated by 1819 through diplomatic means, and Russian pretensions ended by the mid-1820s. An 1818 agreement between the United States and Britain, however, postponed a final boundary determination by granting joint occupancy to the citizens of both nations. The Treaty of 1846 finally fixed the boundary line on paper, but it took another sixteen years to identify what that meant in terms of the land itself. By 1862, surveyors from both countries completed the work of felling trees and placing stakes across the Pacific Northwest's rugged mountain ranges, making it clear when a person stood in one country or the other. British Columbia became part of the new Canadian confederation in 1871, and Washington, Montana, and Idaho became states in 1889–90.

Another 498 miles of the Columbia flow from its headwaters in British Columbia to the 49th parallel.

International Boundary

river mile 745

Plate 168. Seaton's Ferry.
Spokane Public Library
Northwest Room

River Miles Showing Dams and Major Communities

Head of Columbia Lake	1243
Golden	1129
Mica Dam (1973)	956
Revelstoke Dam (1984)	905
Nakusp	862
Keenleyside Dam (1968)	770
International Boundary	745
Kettle Falls	704
Grand Coulee Dam (1941)	597
Chief Joseph Dam (1961)	545
Wells Dam (1967)	515
Rocky Reach Dam (1961)	474
Wenatchee	466
Rock Island Dam (1933)	453
Wanapum Dam (1964)	416
Priest Rapids Dam (1961)	397
Richland	338
Snake River	324
McNary Dam (1957)	292
John Day Dam (1971)	216
The Dalles Dam (1960)	192
Bonneville Dam (1938)	146
Vancouver	102
Longview	66
Astoria	14

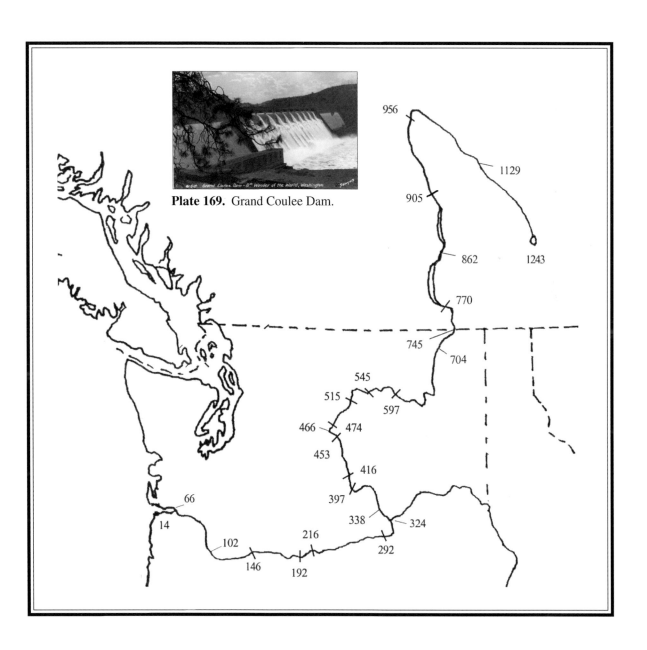

Plate 169. Grand Coulee Dam.

Plate 170. Innomoseecha.
Martha Gamble Collection

184

Principal River Villages ~ circa 1850

Sɪnqi'lt	"above country"
Kɪxkɪus	"trees in the water"
Sxwenítkw	"roaring or noisy water"
N7il7ilmin	"zig-zag flow of water"
Ntcali·'m	"hits the river"
Tkwelwárlweŕxm	"yellowish green plant growth"
Snḵilt	"above the rapids"
Xula'lst	"mountains at the edge of the river"
Npqwiłx	"gray water"
Nəkuktc'iptm	"big basin"
Kali'tcmən	"big rapids"
T'kuya·'tum	"people at the mouth of the river"
Mɛ'txo	"land of sunflower seeds"
Sxa·'tqu	"water pouring out"
Ntià'tku	"weedy river"
Sĭnkŭchĭmuli	"mouth of river"
Kawa'xtcɪn	"living by the banks"
Nqwalqwalmi'n	"roasting place"
P'na	"fish weir"

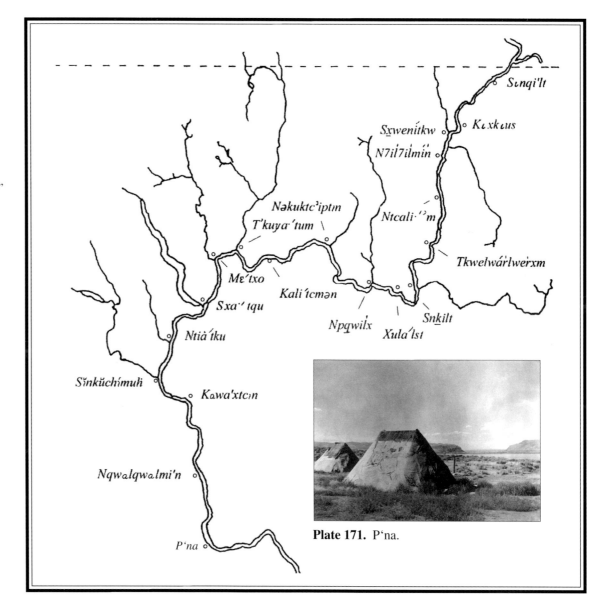

Plate 171. P'na.

185

Plate 172. Brewster band, March 20, 1909.
George Wilson Collection

River Settlements and Towns ~ after 1858

	established	year moved	population (1990 census)
Northport	1892	–	308
Bossburg	1880s	1941	–
Evans	1880s	1941	–
Marcus	1860	1941	135
Kettle Falls	1889	1941	1272
Rice	1883	1941	–
Daisy	1882	1941	10
Gifford	1889	1941	10
Inchelium	–	1941	393
Bissell	1880s	–	10
Cedonia	1858	–	10
Hunters	1880	–	150
Fruitland	1880s	–	75
Gerome	1893	–	0
Peach	1860s	–	0
Lincoln	–	–	–
Plum	1899	–	0
Grand Coulee	1936	–	984
Coulee Dam	1936	–	1,087
Electric City	1887	–	910
Bridgeport	1898	–	1,498
Brewster	1886	–	1,633
Ives Landing (Pateros)	1886	1966	570
Chelan Falls	1893	–	–
Entiat	1887	1905–60	449
Orondo	1884	–	150
Wenatchee	1871	–	21,756
East Wenatchee	–	–	2,701
Rock Island	1888	–	524
Vantage	–	1960	–
Beverly	–	–	–
Mattawa	–	–	941

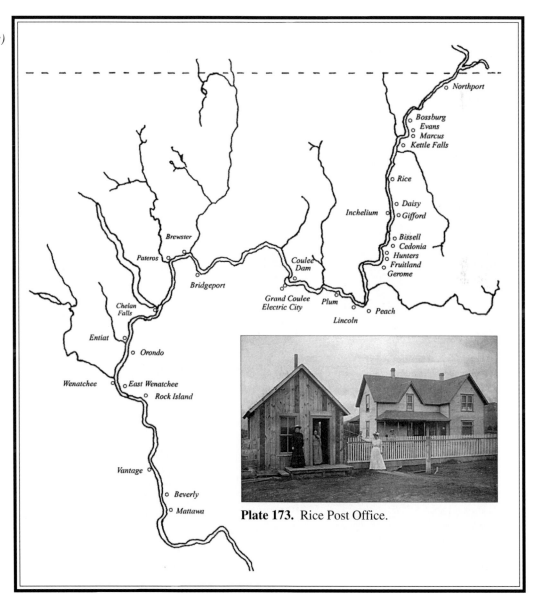

Plate 173. Rice Post Office.

Appendix

Index

About the Author

William D. Layman's passion for the Columbia River began the moment he first saw the river in 1975. Its power, beauty, and mystery have since that time shaped his work as historian, actor, and advocate for placemaking river art. In 1997, he was named one of two first recipients of the James B. Castles Award, given by the Center for Columbia River History. Co-founder of the North Central Washington Playback Theatre Company, Layman's troupe enacts audience stories with historical and other themes using improvisational theatre. In 2001, the company performed at Kettle Falls, where they brought to life memories of older residents who knew the falls prior to their inundation in 1941. In 1996, Layman joined artist Richard Beyer and others in creating a public sculpture of steamboat Captain Alexander Griggs for Wenatchee's Sternwheeler Park. Married with two children, Layman is a resident of Wenatchee where he maintains a private practice in mental health counseling.